GW00983109

# A PRACTICAL GUIDE TO PAYE FOR CHARITIES

## Tax matters relating to staff and volunteers

by Kate Sayer

A Directory of Social Change Publication

# A PRACTICAL GUIDE TO PAYE FOR CHARITIES

Tax matters relating to staff
and volunteers
By Kate Sayer

Published by the Directory of Social Change,
24 Stephenson Way, London NW1 2DP
Copyright 1995 © The Directory of Social Change

No part of this book may be stored in a retrieval
system or reproduced in any form whatsoever without
prior permission in writing from the publishers.

The Directory of Social Change is a registered charity
no. 800517.

ISBN 1873860 33 1

**British Library Cataloguing in Publication Data**
A catalogue record for this book is available from the
British Library

Cover designed by Kate Bass
Designed and typeset by Linda Parker
Printed and bound by Page Bros., Norwich

# Contents

# FOREWORD

This book has been written for charities and voluntary organisations. The rules on taxation and national insurance apply to charities and other employers equally and therefore much of the material in this book could apply to other employers. By the same token, charities could obtain a lot of the information they need from other sources.

This book attempts to bring together the facts and information charities are most likely to need and leaves out much of the information which could only apply to commercial organisations. For example, more time and attention is given to matters such as volunteers.

This book gives only a brief introduction to the basic administration of PAYE. This area is covered extensively in the guides published by the Inland Revenue and the Contributions Agency. I have preferred to concentrate on the areas which most commonly give rise to problems. For those who do need help to get started with a payroll system, then they will find short courses available through the *Council for Voluntary Service* (CVS) network and the *Directory of Social Change*.

A short guide cannot cover every problem the reader may encounter. I apologise if there is something you need which I have missed. I have included a list of reference materials at the back of the book which may give further advice on a particular area. You should not hesitate to contact your local office of the Inland Revenue or Contributions Agency if you are uncertain how to proceed.

Please do write and let me know of your practical experiences, especially if they differ from the situations and examples quoted in the guide. Tax law does keep changing and case law can have a dramatic impact on procedure and practice.

Kate Sayer

Sayer Vincent
23 Angel Gate
City Road
London EC1V 2PT
Tel: 0171-713 0709

6

# ACKNOWLEDGEMENTS

My thanks to Michael Norton for his assistance and editing of this book, also for his patience in waiting for the final version.

I also want to thank all the clients and participants on courses at the Directory of Social Change. Over the years, they asked me questions which sent me searching through reference books. I would never have written this book had they not made me aware of the problems and difficulties faced by charities. They have also provided me with all the examples and case studies.

Staff and colleagues at Sayer Vincent should not be forgotten at this point; they offer encouragement, support and cover for me at the office while I am writing. They have also helped on technical points and collating some of the initial materials to help me get started.

Kate Sayer

# Q U I Z

You may know the answers to some of these questions already, if you have some experience of the PAYE system. You should be able to answer them all by the time you have been through this guide! Suggested answers are at the back of the book.

**1** A small charity pays a cleaner £40 a week to come in and clean their offices. Currently they pay this amount out of petty cash. The administrator takes £40 out of the petty cash tin each Friday, completes and signs the petty cash voucher herself. The voucher just shows the date, the amount and that it was for the cleaner. The administrator leaves the £40 under the kettle for the cleaner to pick up at the weekend.

*What's wrong with this? Suggest improvements to the procedures.*

**2** You take on a part-time employee to help with the bookkeeping. She is receiving a state pension.

*What difference will this make to her tax and national insurance?*

**3** You have a new employee who has recently left school.

*What procedures and forms do you need to follow and what do they need to do?*

**4** You pay someone £500 for a piece of work under the assumption that they were self-employed. It now appears that this may not be the case and you cannot trace the person as they seem to have moved away from the area.

*You have been asked by the trustees to calculate the potential liability for tax and national insurance.*

**5** You have been asked to sort out the final pay for an employee who has been asked to leave without working out their notice. The director of your charity wishes to make the final payment to them as tax effective as possible.

*You look up your records and find that they are owed some holiday pay, some overtime and payment in lieu of notice. Can any of these be paid as ex-gratia payments?*

**6** The management committee wish to help employees travelling a long distance to work and are considering the following options:
a) buying a season ticket for employees
b) making an interest-free loan to employees for the purchase of a season ticket
c) giving employee the cash to buy themselves a season ticket.

*They have asked you to report on the consequences for tax and national insurance of these different options.*

**7** The fundraiser is provided with a car for their work. The car is a Ford Escort and was purchased on 6 May 1994. The following information is available:

| | |
|---|---|
| Manufacturer's price | 13,075 |
| Radio | 575 |
| Sunroof | 255 |
| Number plates | 80 |
| Road fund licence | 105 |
| Delivery | 50 |
| | 14,140 |
| less dealer's discount | (1,300) |
| Cost of purchase | 12,840 |

*Annually, they do over 2,500 miles on charity work. What will the taxable benefit be?*

**8** You also wish to calculate the total cost of the car as above to the employer for inclusion in the budget.

**9** When will employers be able to claim back Statutory Sick Pay in 1995/96?

**10** You wish to pay something to volunteers. How should you deal with this?

# INTRODUCTION

It is a general principle that income tax must be paid by all UK residents on their income. The body of law relating to income tax and other forms of taxation has been built up over the years, and thus has become very complex. In addition to paying income tax, those working have to pay national insurance contributions, which help to pay for pensions, the national health service and social security benefits.

The Pay As You Earn (PAYE) system collects income tax and national insurance contributions from employees at each pay day. Most employees will not have further tax or national insurance to pay and do not have to complete a tax return. The system places the onus on the employer to make the correct deductions for tax and national insurance and to remit these amounts by the due dates to the Inland Revenue. A summary of the amounts due and paid has to be submitted at the end of the tax year.

The PAYE system is only one part of the tax system, and different departments of the Inland Revenue deal with different types of tax. Some of the departments and the terminology which you may come across are:

### H M Inspector of Taxes
The office of the inspector of taxes deals with establishing with taxpayers the amount of tax due to be paid. If you think you are due a refund or a revised coding, then this is the office to contact. Employers are allocated to PAYE inspectors on a geographical basis and are given a reference number. The employee's national insurance (NI) number is needed for any queries about an individual's tax position.

### Collector of Taxes
Once the amount of tax to be collected has been established by the inspector, the papers are passed to the collector. Remittances are sent regularly to a central office in Bradford, but the collector also has local offices. If you are late paying tax, you may be visited by an officer from the local collector's office.

### Schedule D
Self-employed individuals are assessed for income tax under a set of rules known as Schedule D. The rules are different from those applying to employees paying tax through the PAYE system (which is Schedule E).

### Contributions Agency
This is the side of the Department of Social Security dealing with the collection of national insurance. Whilst the PAYE system means that the normal administration and payment of contributions is handled centrally by the Inland Revenue, you will have to contact a different office if you have queries on national insurance, SSP (sick pay) or SMP (maternity pay) matters.

### Claims Branch

Charities reclaiming tax on covenants need to deal with the Inland Revenue Claims Branch, Trusts and Charities Division, based in Bootle, for which they will have a totally separate reference number.

### Corporation Tax

As an organisation, whether a limited company or not, you may be liable to corporation tax. If the organisation is a registered charity, then it is exempt from corporation tax, providing all the income is applied for charitable purposes. The exemption should be confirmed with the charity division in Bootle and the local inspector dealing with corporation tax. If the organisation is a company, than an enquiry form will have been sent automatically from the local inspector of taxes. By supplying them with the appropriate information on the form and in a covering letter, the charitable status for tax purposes should be confirmed for registered charities without any problem. Note that a different reference number will be given for this purpose also. Your organisation will be liable for corporation tax on any profits made from trading activities which are not pursuing the main purpose or incidental fundraising. Your affairs need to be arranged properly to avoid this tax charge.

### PAYE

Pay As You Earn is the system under which the government collects income tax and national insurance by deduction from employees' salaries.

### NI

National Insurance contributions. A specific tax to pay for pensions and national insurance. There is a requirement for minimum contributions if individuals are to qualify for certain benefits. Every individual should have a NI number, and school leavers or immigrants with no previous NI records should obtain a number from the Contributions Agency.

### Basic Rate

Basic rate tax is still 25% (despite the lower rate of 20%), and should be used to make deductions from sub-contractors without form 714. It also applies to those without a tax code.

### Lower Rate

A tax rate of 20% which applies to the first band of taxable earnings (i.e. after personal allowances).

### Higher Rate

A tax rate of 40% which applies to all taxable earnings after a certain threshold has been breached.

### SSP

Statutory Sick Pay. The government scheme to ensure that employees receive a minimum of pay during absences due to sickness.

### SMP

Statutory Maternity Pay. The government scheme to pay women during a period of absence for maternity leave.

### Earnings

Term which has specific meaning in the context of tax and national insurance. Earnings will include payment for work in cash or in kind made to employees.

### Lower Earnings Limit

Term used in national insurance. Those earning less than the limit do not pay national insurance.

### Upper Earnings Limit

Term used in national insurance. Threshold above which employees do not pay national insurance contributions.

### Contracted-out

Employees who are members of an approved pension scheme may be "contracted-out" of the government scheme. They will only receive the flat rate state pension when they reach pensionable age. The employees and employer pay reduced national insurance contributions.

### SERPS

State Earnings Related Pension Scheme. This is the additional pension you receive if you are not contracted-out and make full national insurance contributions throughout your working life.

# CONTACT ADDRESSES

## H M Inspector of Taxes

**For new organisations:** Local office should be contacted by looking under Inland Revenue in the telephone book and ringing the number of the tax enquiry centre which seems nearest. The address of the employer should be quoted and they will give the number of the tax office which deals with that geographical area.

**Existing employers** need to check the documents sent to them (such as the P35) to find the name and address of the tax office they have to deal with. Also reference number (essential for any queries).

## Collector of Taxes

The department responsible for collecting the tax only. Send payments to:

P O Box 1111
Freepost
Bradford
West Yorkshire BD98 8RR

Prepaid envelopes are supplied each year for remitting tax and national insurance.

## Claims Branch

Inland Revenue Claims Branch
(Trusts and Charities)
St John's House
Merton Road
Bootle
Merseyside L69 9BB

Tel: 0151 922 6363

## Contributions Agency

For most queries contact your local social security office, which can be found by looking in your telephone directory under "C". Some matters such as refunds are dealt with by head office:

Department of Social Security
Longbenton
Newcastle upon Tyne NE98 1YX

There is a helpline for employers with queries about national insurance, statutory sick pay and statutory maternity pay:

Tel: 0800 393 539

## Charity Commission

The Charity Commission
St Alban's House
57-60 Haymarket
London SW1Y 4QX

Tel: 0171 210 4477   Fax: 0171 930 9173

The Charity Commission
Second Floor
20 King's Parade
Queen's Dock
Liverpool L3 4DQ

Tel: 0151 703 1500   Fax: 0151 703 1555

The Charity Commission
Woodfield House
Tangier
Taunton
Somerset TA1 4BL

Tel: 01823 345000   Fax: 01823 345003

The Charity Commission advises charities on various matters concerning management and good practice. The permission of the Charity Commission must be sought if trustees wish to make ex- gratia payments or pay trustees.

## NCVO

National Council for Voluntary Organisations
Regent's Wharf
8 All Saint's Street
London N1 9RL

Tel: 0171 713 6161   Fax: 0171 713 6300

Membership organisation for national voluntary organisations in England, providing advice and support. Local organisations should contact their local Council for Voluntary Service (CVS).

## SCVO

Scottish Council for Voluntary Organisations
18-19 Claremont Crescent
Edinburgh EH7 4QD

Tel: 0131 556 3882  Fax: 0131 556 0279

Membership organisation for voluntary organisations in Scotland, providing advice and support.

## WCVA

Wales Council for Voluntary Action
Llys Ifor
Crescent Road
Caerffili
Mid-Glamorgan CF8 1XL

Tel: 0222 869224   Fax: 0222 860627

Membership organisation for voluntary organisations in Wales, providing advice and support.

## Volunteer Centre

The Volunteer Centre UK
Carriage Row
183 Eversholt Street
London NW1 1BU

Tel: 0171 388 9888   Fax: 0171 383 0448

Advise on all aspects of volunteering and publish booklets on the subject.

## DSC

The Directory of Social Change
Radius Works
Back Lane
London NW3 1HL

Tel: 0171 431 1817   Fax: 0171 794 7724

Publish books and guides on management, finance and fundraising for the charity and voluntary sector. Also run courses and seminars on relevant subjects.

## NACVS

National Association of Councils for Voluntary Service
Arundel Court
Arundel Street
Sheffield S1 2NU

Tel: 01742 786636   Fax: 01742 787004

Produce a guide to all courses being run by CVS's in the UK.

## CAF

Charities Aid Foundation
48 Pembury Road
Tonbridge
Kent TN9 2JD

Tel: 01732 771333   Fax: 01732 350570

Mainly concerned with fundraising and operates a payroll giving service (tax effective donations deducted from employees' gross pay).

# Chapter 1

# BASICS OF THE PAYE SYSTEM

The tax year runs from 6 April to 5 April the following year. An individual, a company, an unincorporated association, a charitable trust or any body however constituted may be an employer.

If you pay individuals for work they do, then you are probably an employer and must register with the local tax office. Telephone the nearest Inland Revenue office listed in the telephone directory and check whether they cover your area. They will take a few details and send you a starter pack.

You must then keep records of the amounts paid to employees and deduct the correct amounts of tax and national insurance, sending the deductions to the Collector of Taxes. They will provide you with payslips and envelopes for sending in the amounts due.

## TAX CODES

Every UK resident is entitled to a certain amount of tax free income each tax year. The basic entitlement is the personal allowance. People over a certain age receive a higher personal allowance ("age allowance") and additional allowances are available for those living with a child, married couples and blind persons. The amount of tax free pay to which an individual is entitled is reflected in the tax code. The tax code may be adjusted to reduce the free pay so that tax is collected on benefits received in kind or for earlier unpaid tax bills. Each individual may check their code with their tax office (quoting their national insurance number) and receive a notice of coding detailing the way in which it has been calculated. It is up to the individual to notify the tax office if their circumstances change, for example, if they marry.

The employer must use the code they are given by the tax office. This is usually notified on a form P9 Notice of Coding. The employer may not change the code without a notice, even if they know that there is something wrong. The employer or employee must contact the tax office and advise them of the problem and obtain a new code. Employers should keep the notices of coding they receive as proof that they are applying the correct code.

Details of how to use the codes in conjunction with the Pay Adjustment Tables are given in the Employer's Basic Guide to PAYE (cards P8) sent with the starter pack. There are also instructions at the beginning of the Pay Adjustment Tables on their use. The tables give you the amount of total free pay to date in the tax year, which is deducted from the gross pay to date to calculate the taxable pay to date. Computerised systems will contain the equivalent of the tables on master files and, providing the current tables are installed and the correct code entered, the calculations will be undertaken automatically as part of the payroll run.

---

### Allowances – Annual Amount of Tax-Free Pay

| | 1994/95 | 1995/96 | Notes |
|---|---|---|---|
| Single person allowance | £3,445 | £3,525 | |
| Additional allowance (for married men or person with a dependent child) | £1,720 | £1,720 | relief restricted to 20% |
| Age allowance – single | £4,200 | £4,630 | for those aged 65-74 |
| Age allowance – additional | £2,665 | £2,995 | for married men aged 65-74; relief restricted to 20% |
| Age allowance – single | £4,370 | £4,800 | over 75 years old |
| Age allowance – additional | £2,705 | £3,035 | over 75 years old; relief restricted to 20% |
| Blind person's allowance | £1,200 | £1,200 | additional |

---

A married man would be entitled to both the single personal allowance and the additional allowance, £5,165 in total in 1994/95. But new rules in 1994/95 mean that the extent of relief available for the additional personal allowance is limited to only 20% in 1994/95. So the value of the additional personal allowance is £1,720 x 20% = £344. A married man receives a reduction in his tax bill of £344.

The additional personal allowance is also available to a single person with a dependant child. In the case of an unmarried couple with a child, it may be split between the two parents or allocated to just the one parent as they choose. The tax code is adjusted to ensure that the correct amount of allowances is given. In a similar way, a married couple may jointly elect to share the allowance between them or transfer the whole amount to the wife.

Note that the value of the additional personal allowance is reduced for 1995/96, as the tax relief is restricted to 15%.

## Mortgage Interest Relief

An individual can obtain tax relief on the interest payable on a loan (maximum £30,000) for the purchase of their main or only residence. This relief will normally be shared equally if the property is in shared ownership, such as a couple buying their home in joint names, although they can opt for a different allocation of the relief. Usually this tax relief is calculated by the bank or building society and given at source, so that the mortgage repayments made are reduced for the tax relief. This is known as MIRAS – Mortgage Interest Relief At Source. Most employees obtain tax relief under this scheme by completing a form when they take out the mortgage. Only employees not on MIRAS will need to complete details on their tax return and obtain relief through an increase in their tax code.

Note that the value of this relief is decreasing. The relief is restricted to 20% in 1994/95 and to 15% in 1995/96. There is no need for employers to do anything as changes will be effected through the amount repayable on the mortgage for MIRAS taxpayers, or through the tax code for others.

---

### Example – Mortgage Interest Relief

Janet and John have a mortgage of £65,000 and they will make repayments to the building society of £5,600 in this tax year. The total interest charge for the year is £5,200 They will not get tax relief on the total interest charge, but only on interest on a £30,000 loan:

$$£5,200 \times \frac{£30,000}{£65,000} = £2,400$$

In 1994/95 the amount of the tax relief will be restricted to a 20% rate:

$$£2,400 \times 20\% = £480$$

So the repayments Janet and John make will be:

| | |
|---|---|
| capital repayment | 880 |
| interest | 5,200 |
| less tax relief | (480) |
| | 5,600 |

In 1995/96 the amount of tax relief will be restricted to a 15% rate. So assuming the interest charge remains the same:

$$£2,400 \times 15\% = £360$$

Repayments Janet and John make will have to be increased

| | |
|---|---|
| capital repayment | 880 |
| interest | 5,200 |
| less tax relief | (360) |
| | 5,720 |

The building society will ask them to increase their monthly payment accordingly.

---

## Other deductions for tax purposes

Employees may be able to claim additional allowances against gross pay, which will usually be reflected in their tax code. For example, payments to an approved personal pension plan will usually be eligible for tax relief. The employee has to submit details to the tax office to obtain a changed tax code.

The basic rule for qualifying deductions is that they should be incurred "wholly, exclusively and necessarily" in the performance of duties. Travel expenses should be "necessarily" incurred. The deduction should be claimed by the employee on a tax return. If allowances for these expenses are declared on a P11D (Return of Expenses and Benefits) by the employer, then the employee should claim a deduction for the actual amount of the expenses.

Travel expenses are examined in more detail in the chapter on "Benefits".

## Subscriptions

Subscriptions to a professional body or to a journal may qualify for tax relief. To qualify the employee should be obliged to subscribe because of the nature of their work. The employee has to pay the subscription from his or her own funds. The subscriptions to professional bodies which qualify for tax relief are listed in a handbook. If the employer pays the subscriptions, then no claim can be made by the employee.

## Emergency Code

The emergency code is the code used when a new employee starts work with you and they do not have a form P45 from their previous employment. To use the emergency code they should have no other job. It will give them the same amount of tax free pay as the single personal allowance, but it is not used on a cumulative basis as normal. It is used on a week 1 or month 1 basis. This means that you just calculate the gross pay each week or month, deduct the tax free pay according to the Pay Adjustment Tables week 1 or month 1 and look up the tax payable. Full instructions on the application of the emergency code are given in the employer's Basic Guide to PAYE (Cards P8).

## "K" Codes

Certain employees may receive valuable benefits in kind or receive other income such as a pension. These may exceed the amount of the personal allowances due to them, so that they effectively should have a negative code. These are the "K" codes and there are special tables supplied to every employer for the proper application of the "K" codes. If an employee has a "K"code, then you should add this amount to their gross pay to arrive at their taxable pay.

## Tax Rates

The basic rate of tax is 25% (1994/95) and has been the same for the last seven years. For 1994/95, this rate of tax applies to taxable income between the amounts £3,001 and £23,700. For 1995/96 the 25% band applies to taxable income between the amounts £3,201 and £24,300.

The lower rate of tax of 20% was introduced in 1992/93 and in 1994/95 applies to the first £3,000 of taxable income. In 1995/96 the 20% band will apply to the first £3,200 of taxable income.

The higher rate of tax is 40% and applies to all taxable income above £23,700 in 1994/95. In 1995/96, the 40% band applies to all taxable income above £23,300.

The Taxable Pay Tables will produce the correct calculations on a month by month basis if you follow the instructions carefully. Computerised systems will produce the correct tax payable figure providing the tax rates for the correct tax year are loaded.

### Example – Tax Rates

Jane is a single person earning £30,000 gross per year in 1994/95 She has no extra tax reliefs or taxable benefits. How much tax should she pay?

|  | £ |
|---|---|
| Gross pay | 30,000 |
| less Personal Allowance (total free pay) | (3,445) |
| Taxable income | 26,555 |

| | |
|---|---|
| Tax due on £3,000 @ 20% | 600 |
| Tax due on next £20,700 @ 25% | 5,175 |
| Tax due on next £2,855 (£26,555-£23,700) @ 40% | 1,142 |
| Total tax due | 6,917 |

# Basic Rate Tax

There will be situations where you are instructed to use the basic rate against someone's earnings, for example if you employ someone who has another job. You must use 25%, even if you think they may be entitled to pay lower rate tax. Any adjustment necessary will be made by the tax office at the end of the tax year and a refund will be paid to the employee direct if appropriate. Alternatively, the tax office will supply you with a notice of coding if the tax code is to be split between the employments.

# Payroll Giving

Employers who operate payroll giving make the deductions from the employee's gross pay and pay the donation over to an agent. An employee may donate up to £900 per year from gross pay. There is no change to the limit in 1995/96.

# National Insurance

There are two aspects of national insurance contributions for employed people: the employee's contribution and the employer's contribution. The employee's contribution is deducted from gross pay and paid over to the Inland Revenue together with the tax deducted. The employer's contribution is a cost to the employer only, and is also calculated as a percentage of the gross pay. This also has to be paid at the same time to the Inland Revenue.

For most people the standard rates of national insurance are:

|  | 1994/95 rates | 1995/96 rates |
|---|---|---|
| Employee's Contribution | 10% | 10% |
| Employer's Contribution | 10.2% | 10.2% |

For 1994/95, a lower rate of employee's contribution of only 2% applies to the first £57 per week or £247 per month. Additionally, employees do not have to contribute any more once their earnings reach the maximum threshold of £430 per week or £1,864 per month. The employer's contributions are graduated for earnings of less than £200 per week or £867 per month. The details of the rates applicable to any particular tax year are given at the front of the National Insurance Tables (Tables 1) which are sent automatically to every employer registered for PAYE.

These contributions are for those contracted in to the state pension scheme. There are different rates where the employer runs their own occupational pension scheme, for which you need the tables for contracted-out contributions. You may not use these tables unless you are part of an approved pension scheme and therefore have a contracted out number.

National Insurance Contributions are described in "classes", as different categories and rates do apply in different situations. All employees and employers have to pay Class 1 contributions, as described above. The other categories are:

- ◆ **Class 1A**
  National insurance contributions payable on the private use of cars and fuel provided by an employer to an employee

- ◆ **Class 2**
  Flat rate contributions payable by self- employed individuals

- ◆ **Class 3**
  Voluntary contributions payable by those working abroad or not in full-time employment

- ◆ **Class 4**
  Payable by the self-employed in addition to Class 2 and calculated as a percentage of profits

Payment of Class 1 national insurance entitles individuals to unemployment benefit, statutory sick pay, statutory maternity pay and State Earnings Related Pension Scheme (SERPS). Self employed people are only entitled to certain other benefits such as the basic pension. Further information about Class 1, Class 1A and Class 3 contributions is given in Chapter 5. Class 2 and Class 4 contributions are beyond the scope of this book, as they refer to self-employed individuals. Leaflets CA02 and CA03 available from the Contributions Agency will give you further information in this area.

It is important that the end of year return (P14) is correctly completed and submitted for all employees. The employee's record of contributions will be updated from the P14 and will form the basis of any check for subsequent claims for benefit or pension. The employee's national insurance number must be correctly stated on the end of year return. Queries about individual's contribution records have to be directed to the Contributions Agency main office in Newcastle.

## Remitting to the Inland Revenue

Each month, employers must send in the tax and national insurance they have deducted from employees. They must also include the employer's national insurance contributions. Amounts may be withheld by the employer for Statutory Sick Pay in certain circumstances and Statutory Maternity Pay. *(For further details, see Chapter 7 on Sick pay and Maternity pay.)*

You need to summarise the totals due for all employees, weekly and monthly paid. The total amount of tax and national insurance due for the month should be entered on the payslip provided and remitted to the Inland Revenue Accounts Office by the 19th of the month following payday.

---

### Example – Remitting to the Inland Revenue

You have summarised the payroll for the month of April in a salaries book. This shows the following totals:

|  | £ |
|---|---|
| Tax | 3,405.76 |
| Employees' NI | 3,098.75 |
| Employer's NI | 1,075.46 |
| Total due | 7,579.97 |
| *Less* SMP | 574.48 |
| Net due | 7,005.49 |

This amount should be paid to the Inland Revenue by 19 May.

---

## Quarterly Remittances

Small employers may choose to remit tax and national insurance to the Inland Revenue quarterly instead of monthly. To qualify as a 'small employer', total tax and national insurance should be less than £450 per month. To change to quarterly remittances, apply to the Inland Revenue Accounts Office at Bradford.

## RECORDS AND DOCUMENTATION

The employer is obliged to keep certain records for PAYE purposes and to provide employees with certain documentation. PAYE records have to be kept for three years after the end of the tax year to which they relate. Since tax cases stay open for six years, however, it may be wise to keep records for six years. On the whole, you will be complying with the law if you complete the forms supplied to you by the Inland Revenue, or substitute forms containing the same information. If you operate a computerised payroll, then similar records should be maintained as part of the system. Most packages which you buy off the shelf will incorporate adequate records for PAYE purposes.

## Deductions Working Sheet and Payslips

The Deductions Working Sheet (P11) is the individual pay record showing gross pay, taxable pay calculations and deductions. It also shows SSP, SMP and national insurance. You should ensure that you are using the current version of the form as it is amended from time to time to reflect new rules.

A payslip must be given to every employee every payday. This must show as a minimum:

♦ gross pay

♦ description and amounts of all deductions

◆ net pay

◆ if different parts of the net amount are paid in different ways, the amount and method of each part payment The records and documentation above are required by law. Additionally, certain records are useful as they summarise information and assist in the accounting function. To operate good internal controls, you may also wish to use some forms and procedures suggested below.

## Salary summary or wages book

As well as the individual records, it is useful to summarise the gross pay, deductions and net pay for each payday. This can be used to double check that the correct amount of net pay has been paid in total and to total the amounts due to the Inland Revenue. It can also form the basis for entries into the accounting system. Where it applies, the summary can identify the department or cost centre where an employee works and prepare information on staff costs in a useful manner for accounting purposes.

## P32

The Inland Revenue supply this record, although its use is optional. It is a preprinted record for payments due and made to the Inland Revenue for the tax year. Employers with only a couple of employees may find that they can use this instead of a wages book to summarise the information they need. It is useful when preparing the end of year summary.

## End of year summaries

At the end of the tax year the totals from the P11's have to be entered on forms P14. You must complete one for each employee. These forms are three-part sets and the top two copies should be sent to the Inland Revenue with the Employer's Summary (P35). The third copy is a form P60 and should be handed to the employee. It is wise to keep your own copies of these forms if you operate a manual system, so that you can refer to them in the event of a query. These forms are usually produced as part of the end of year routine on computerised systems, so you should just make sure that you have back up copies of the data in whatever form is most convenient. It is possible to submit end of year information on computer disk or magnetic tape if you wish, but you should obtain clearance in advance.

## Other information

Other forms and information you should keep

◆ Part 3 of forms P45 for employees joining in the tax year

◆ notices of coding received

◆ completed forms P46 for employees paid below the threshold for tax and national insurance

◆ names and addresses of any casual employees

♦ copies of forms P38(S) for students

♦ sickness records (for periods of sickness of four days or more)

♦ maternity leave details

You will be asked to produce these forms when you have a PAYE or Social Security audit visit. Set up a good filing system which keeps the records for each tax year separately.

## OTHER DEDUCTIONS

Employers may need to make other deductions from employees' pay in addition to tax and national insurance. Examples include:

♦ loan repayments

♦ union dues

♦ payroll giving contributions to charity

♦ pension contributions (superannuation)

♦ advances of salary

Permission to make deductions must be obtained from the employee before the event which causes the deductions to be made. For example, an employer makes a loan to an employee for the purchase of a car. Before the loan has been made and the car purchased, the employee should sign a loan agreement and repayment schedule, authorising the employer to make deductions from the employee's net pay. If the agreement and authorisation are signed after the loan has already been made, then the employee may have grounds for claiming that the deductions are not being made legally.

Consequently, it is important that proper documentation is drawn up and signed at the right time. This should show the authorisation for the deduction to be made e.g. loan agreement and repayment schedule, specifying that the repayments will be made by deduction from net pay. The deductions should be shown clearly on the payslip. To ensure that authorisation for deductions does exist, a clause should be inserted into the contract of employment to cover this.

## RECTIFYING MISTAKES

Problems can arise when mistakes have been made and the employer needs to recover an overpayment to an employee. The general principle is that mistakes of fact may be rectified and the employee asked to repay the amount. Mistakes in interpreting the law which result in an overpayment to an employee may only be recovered from the employee with their consent. It is not always straightforward to apply this principle.

### Some examples
1. An overtime payment is paid to the wrong employee.

2. You do not deduct PAYE from someone's pay because you thought you did not have to.

3. You mistakenly pay Statutory Maternity Pay to an employee in addition to their full wages.

### Answers

1. This is an error of fact and should be recoverable from the employee.

2. This is more likely to be an error of law – you did not understand how the law applied to this situation and the overpayment cannot be recovered. If the employee deliberately misled you as to their status, then it is more likely that they can be said to have contributed to the error and therefore the overpayment would be recoverable.

3. This is an error of law and the overpayment cannot be recovered unless the employee agrees to it.

The answers to the above examples could be more complicated, depending on the actual sequence of events. To extend the story in example 1, let us suppose the employee went to the employer and notified them that they thought a mistake had been made. The employer confirms that no mistake has been made and that the pay is correct. In these circumstances, the employee may well be entitled to claim that they had relied upon this representation and acted accordingly, spending all the money. It would therefore not be fair to ask them subsequently to repay the overpayment. (The facts are similar to those in a case R E Jones Ltd v. Waring and Gillow Ltd.)

An employer may wish to make a deduction from an employee's pay because of absence or another aspect of non-performance. This may not be legal and the employee may be able to go to an industrial tribunal to have the pay restituted. For example, a case heard by the tribunal where an employee left without giving notice ruled that the employer had to pay wages which they had withheld for breach of contract. Similar situations could arise where an employee is absent for long periods or does not notify sickness in the proper manner. You need to check contracts of employment to ensure that the right to withhold pay is specifically dealt with, as well as the circumstances in which such a sanction may apply. The employer may be entitled to withhold pay in cases of breach of contract, but this has to be part of the contractual conditions.

In situations where a significant amount of money is involved, then it is wise to seek legal advice. Trustees of charities need to exercise great care to ensure that they are not negligent in safeguarding the assets of the charity. Mistakes could mean that proper checks and controls are not in place. Since this is the responsibility of the trustees, they may be held personally liable if significant amounts of the charity's funds are lost through negligence.

---

### Action Points: PAYE and Deductions

**1.** Check that all tables for PAYE calculations are the up to date versions.

**2.** Make a note of the tax office address and reference number in a safe place.

**3.** Make sure that you pay over tax and national insurance promptly by 19th of month following. Put a reminder in your diary or on your wall planner!

**4.** For each tax year, make a list of employees and their national insurance numbers. This will make the returns at the end of year easier to prepare and you will not omit employees who have left during the year.

**5.** Ensure that you have a good stock of forms: P11, P45, P46, P14, P38 (S), SSP forms, SMP forms.

**6.** Prepare Employer's Summary (P35) promptly after year end and submit before 19 May to avoid interest on late payment of tax and national insurance.

**7.** Check contracts of employment include a clause allowing the employer to make deductions for loan repayments, the return of expenses floats, etc.

## SOME PAYE FORMS AND THEIR USES

| | |
|---|---|
| P8 | Employer's Basic Guide to PAYE on a set of cards, which are updated as necessary and sent to all employers operating PAYE. |
| P9 | Notification of coding sent to the employer when an employee's code has been changed or is confirmed. |
| P9D | Return of Expenses and Benefits form for employees earning at a rate below £8,500. |
| P11 | Deductions Working Sheet. One form for each employee to show their earnings, tax and national insurance calculations on a month by month (or week by week) basis over the tax year. |
| P11D | Return of Employees Expenses and Benefits. Form has to be completed by employer each year to show benefits, such as private use of car, private health insurance. |
| P11D(b) | Form to be completed and submitted by employer to confirm that all necessary forms P9D and P11D have been completed and submitted. |
| P14 | End of Year Summary. A form P14 has to be completed for each employee and shows the totals for the tax year from the P11 Deductions Working Sheet. The forms P14 have to be submitted with the P35. They come as a multipart form containing three copies. Two have to be sent to the Inland Revenue and a third copy is given to the employee and is called a P60. |
| P32 | Summary of the tax and national insurance due month by month, with space to note date of remittance to the Inland Revenue. Optional – useful for small employers. |
| P35 | Employer's Summary (End of Year Return). This form is used to total all the tax and national insurance due for all employees in a tax year. The form also requires the amount paid over to the Inland Revenue to be entered, so that a final amount due is calculated. |

P38A Supplementary Return to be submitted at the end of the tax year if anyone has been paid more than £100 cash without deduction of tax or national insurance because they were employed by you for less than one week on a casual basis.

**P38(S)**    Student Employed During Holidays – if the student signs this form, then there is no need to deduct tax.

**P45**    Details of Employee Leaving. Form to be completed in full by employer when employee leaves. Part 1 is sent to tax office; Parts 2 and 3 given to the leaver. New employees should bring these with them and new employer keeps Part 2 and sends in Part 3 to their tax office.

**P46**    Form used when new employee does not bring Parts 2 & 3 of P45 with them. P46 asks whether they have other jobs and has to be signed by employee.

**P60**    Certificate of Tax and National Insurance. This is a summary of the gross pay, tax, national insurance and other details which the employer should give to every employee at the end of the tax year. The form is part of a multipart set together with the P14, so the information is identical to the information sent in to the Inland Revenue at the end of the tax year.

**714**    Subcontractors certificate exempting them from having tax deducted at source. If a builder, decorator or other organisation in the construction industry can produce a certificate 714, then you may pay them gross.

| Deductions Working Sheet P11 | Year to 5 April 19 |
|---|---|

Employer's name

Tax District and reference

Complete only for occupational pension schemes newly contracted-out since 1 January 1986.
Scheme contracted-out number

| S | 4 | | | | | | | |
|---|---|---|---|---|---|---|---|---|

| Employee's surname *in CAPITALS* | | First two forenames | |
|---|---|---|---|
| National Insurance no. | Date of birth *in figures* Day Month Year | Works no. etc | Date of leaving *in figures* Day Month Year |

| Tax code † | Amended code † | | | | |
|---|---|---|---|---|---|
| | Wk/Mth in which applied | | | | |

**National Insurance contributions*** / **PAYE Income Tax**

| For employer's use | Earnings on which employee's contributions payable 1a | Total of employee's and employer's contributions payable 1b | Employee's contributions payable 1c | Earnings on which employee's contributions at contracted-out rate payable included in column 1a 1d | Employee's contributions at contracted-out rate included in column 1c 1e | Statutory Sick Pay in the week or month included in column 2 1f | Statutory Maternity Pay in the week or month included in column 2 1g | Statutory Maternity Pay recovered 1h | Month no | Week no | Pay in the week or month including Statutory Sick Pay/Statutory Maternity Pay 2 | Total pay to date 3 | Total free pay to date (Table A) 4a | K codes only: Total 'additional pay' to date (Table A) 4b | Total taxable pay to date i.e. column 3 *minus* column 4a or column 3 *plus* column 4b 5 | Total tax due to date as shown by Taxable Pay Tables 6 | K codes only: Tax due at end of current period Mark refunds 'R' 6a | K codes only: Regulatory limit i.e. 50% of column 2 entry 6b | Tax deducted or refunded in the week or month. Mark refunds 'R' 7 | K codes only: Tax not deducted owing to the Regulatory limit 8 | For employer's use |
|---|---|---|---|---|---|---|---|---|---|---|---|---|---|---|---|---|---|---|---|---|---|
| | £ | £ | £ | £ | £ | £ | £ | £ | | | £ | £ | £ | £ | £ | £ | £ | £ | £ | £ | |
| | | | | | | | | | | 1 | | | | | | | | | | | |
| | | | | | | | | | | 2 | | | | | | | | | | | |
| | | | | | | | | | | 3 | | | | | | | | | | | |
| | | | | | | | | | 1 | 4 | | | | | | | | | | | |
| | | | | | | | | | | 5 | | | | | | | | | | | |
| | | | | | | | | | | 6 | | | | | | | | | | | |
| | | | | | | | | | | 7 | | | | | | | | | | | |
| | | | | | | | | | 2 | 8 | | | | | | | | | | | |
| | | | | | | | | | | 9 | | | | | | | | | | | |
| | | | | | | | | | | 10 | | | | | | | | | | | |
| | | | | | | | | | | 11 | | | | | | | | | | | |
| | | | | | | | | | | 12 | | | | | | | | | | | |
| | | | | | | | | | 3 | 13 | | | | | | | | | | | |
| | | | | | | | | | | 14 | | | | | | | | | | | |
| | | | | | | | | | | 15 | | | | | | | | | | | |
| | | | | | | | | | | 16 | | | | | | | | | | | |
| | | | | | | | | | 4 | 17 | | | | | | | | | | | |
| | | | | | | | | | | 18 | | | | | | | | | | | |
| | | | | | | | | | | 19 | | | | | | | | | | | |
| | | | | | | | | | | 20 | | | | | | | | | | | |
| | | | | | | | | | 5 | 21 | | | | | | | | | | | |
| | | | | | | | | | | 22 | | | | | | | | | | | |
| | | | | | | | | | | 23 | | | | | | | | | | | |
| | | | | | | | | | | 24 | | | | | | | | | | | |
| | | | | | | | | | | 25 | | | | | | | | | | | |
| | | | | | | | | | 6 | 26 | | | | | | | | | | | |
| | | | | | | | | | | 27 | | | | | | | | | | | |
| | | | | | | | | | | 28 | | | | | | | | | | | |
| | | | | | | | | | | 29 | | | | | | | | | | | |
| | | | | | | | | | 7 | 30 | | | | | | | | | | | |
| | Total c/fwd | Total c/fwd | Total c/fwd | Total c/fwd | Total c/fwd | Total c/fwd | Total c/fwd | Total c/fwd | | | | | | | | | | | | | |

P11(1995)

* You must enter the NI contribution table letter overleaf beside the NI totals box - *see the note shown there.*

† If amended cross out previous code.

∅ If any week/month the amount in column 4a is more than the amount in column 3, leave column 5 blank.

## PAYSLIP SAMPLE

### THE GOOD CHARITY EMPLOYER

Model Employee

Code:  344L

NI:  AZ60 43 20 Z

Week / Month:

| | | |
|---|---|---|
| Gross pay for month | | |
| Tax deducted | | |
| NI deducted | | |
| NET PAY | | |
| Other deductions | | |
| PAYMENT BY CHEQUE | | |

# SALARIES BOOK SAMPLE

Month: July

| Name | Gross | Employee's Pension Cont'n | Tax | Employee's NI | Net Pay | Employer's NI | SSP | SMP |
|---|---|---|---|---|---|---|---|---|
| Jane B | 1,500.00 | – | 290.75 | 145.44 | 1063.81 | 153.00 | – | – |
| Jim H. | 1,233.33 | – | 195.41 | 118.77 | 919.15 | 125.80 | – | – |
| Abdul S. | 1,233.33 | – | 224.08 | 118.77 | 890.48 | 125.80 | – | – |
| Maria T. | 833.33 | – | 124.08 | 78.77 | 630.48 | 85.00 | | |
| TOTALS FOR MONTH | 4,799.99 | – | 834.32 | 461.75 | 3503.92 | 489.60 | | |

## LIST OF EMPLOYEES SAMPLE

| Name | NI Number | Started | Left | Notes |
|---|---|---|---|---|
| Jane Banks | XY 23 46 57 Z | – | 7 July | P11D |
| Jim Howden | AB 45 78 93 C | 1 May | | P11D |
| Abdul Shah | CD 54 93 12 E | – | – | P11D |
| Maria Tzintakis | EF 27 64 78 H | – | – | no P11D |
| | | | | |
| | | | | |
| | | | | |
| | | | | |
| | | | | |

Chapter 2

# WHO IS AN EMPLOYEE?

One of the most important basic questions you need to understand is that of employee status. Many people would like to avoid the administration and cost of the PAYE system and therefore look for ways round the fact of employment. This will not always be so cost-effective. The Inland Revenue undertake audit visits, collate records centrally and keep files open for six years. When they visit, they specifically ask to see cash books and petty cash records. They will look at payments to individuals and examine invoices supplied. They can determine that you should have treated someone as an employee and deducted tax and national insurance under the PAYE system when you paid them. Not only would you (or the organisation) have to pay over the tax and national insurance which should have been deducted, but there may also be penalties for non-compliance with the law.

## EMPLOYEE STATUS

An employer-employee relationship will probably exist if the majority of the following conditions apply:

◆ a contract of employment exists

◆ the person undertakes the work on the employer's premises

◆ the person is contracted to work regular hours

◆ the person is paid a rate for the hours worked

◆ the person uses equipment supplied by the employer

◆ the person is paid for holidays and sick leave

◆ the person's work is controlled by the employer

What constitutes an employment is a legal minefield; there have been many cases in the courts which have focused on the question of employee status. The Inland Revenue will look at the overall situation to determine whether they think the person undertaking work for you is an employee or not. It would not be necessary for all the above conditions to be fulfilled. You might employ someone on a short term contract and agree not to pay them holiday pay or sick pay. You may employ people who work in their own home using their own equipment.

### Self-Employed Personnel

Situations where the question is most likely to arise is where you have the option or are requested to treat someone as self- employed rather than an employee. The following conditions would need to exist for a person to be treated as a self-employed person rather then employed:

- ◆ the person should be in business on their own account and therefore at risk of making a loss (as well as a profit)
- ◆ the person would probably be paid a fee for the job, rather than a fee for certain hours
- ◆ the person would control their work, within the agreed instructions
- ◆ there would be no holiday or sickness pay
- ◆ the person supplies their own materials and equipment
- ◆ the person undertakes work for more than one person
- ◆ there would be a contract for services
- ◆ another person may be used to carry out the designated tasks

Of these, the first condition is the really important one. All the others are subsidiary points, which confirm the fact that the person is in business on their own account.

## What sort of work?

The situation may arise where a self-employed person is contracted by your organisation to undertake work for you which is in the nature of employment. If the organisation is offering employment with terms and conditions which accompany that, then the person will be an employee for that particular job and should be treated as such for tax purposes. It is quite possible for someone to have a part-time job and to be self-employed for other assignments. The fact alone that they work for many employers does not make them self-employed; they may have two or more part- time jobs. It is essential that you are clear about the terms and conditions applying to the position.

### Example 1

Jo is an actress, but when she has no acting work she works as a temporary secretary. She has self-employed status for all her acting work.

Her self-employed status will not necessarily extend to her secretarial work. If your organisation offers her a temporary position where she will be working on your premises, at your direction, using your equipment and paid an hourly rate, then this should be treated as temporary employment and her earnings paid through the PAYE system.

### Example 2

You see a small ad in the local newspaper, advertising secretarial services. You discover that Dee works from home and will collect and deliver typing.

Dee is set up in business on her own account and you may buy her services without taking her on as an employee. However, you would change that status if you offered her a job one day a week working at your office.

## Self-Employed v. Employed

A great number of people believe that they are better off if they are self employed. This is not necessarily the case! A self- employed person may be able to deduct some of their expenses against their earnings, but these still have to be legitimate business expenses. They may have to use the services of an accountant to assist them with their accounts and tax return. They are not paid when ill or on holiday; they have to pay for their own training and undertake training in their own time. They often have to agree to a fixed fee for a piece of work and may have to spend much longer to complete the work than anticipated. They do pay lower national insurance contributions, but then they receive lower levels of benefit. For example, unemployment, sickness, pensions and maternity benefits are all substantially lower if you are self-employed. Savings or some form of private provision for all these will probably be needed.

Employees do benefit from a certain amount of legal protection of their rights, which self-employed people obviously miss. Someone who has been employed by the same employer for a minimum of two years is entitled to statutory redundancy pay and may take an employer to an industrial tribunal if they feel they have been unfairly dismissed. Most of the employee protection legislation now applies to part-time employees as well as full-time employees.

It does, of course, cost employers more to use employees rather than self-employed personnel. The main consideration is that employer's national insurance contributions have to be paid. The employee's salary rate cannot be adjusted to take this into consideration, whereas the freelance rate and the employee rate can be equalised for benefits such as holiday pay.

### Example

You agree to use the services of a consultant for an organisational review. The consultant has agreed to be paid at the equivalent of the deputy director's salary of £20,000 per annum. The deputy director's terms and conditions allows for five weeks holiday plus the bank holidays.

| | |
|---|---:|
| Total number of working days in the year | 260 |
| Less   holidays- five weeks per year | (25) |
| statutory days – bank holidays | (8) |
| Days available for work | 227 |

£20,000 divided by 227 days = £88.11 per day

The consultant should be paid at a daily rate of £88.11 per day.

The actual cost to the organisation of employing the deputy director is the daily rate plus the employer's national insurance. The actual cost of employing the consultant will be the daily rate only.

## Getting it wrong

Remember, if you mistakenly pay someone gross because you thought they were self-employed, but the Inland Revenue disagree with this view, then the amount paid to that person will be assumed to be the net pay. In the example above, we calculated the daily rate of £88.11 for the consultant on the basis of gross pay. If this is deemed to be the net pay, then the Inland Revenue will demand to collect tax and national insurance as follows:

£88.11 equivalent to net pay assumes deductions of 25% tax and 10% employee's national insurance. Therefore gross pay should have been £88.11 divided by 65 and multiplied by 100, which is £135.55.

The tax and national insurance payable will be:

| | |
|---|---|
| Tax at 25% of £135.55 | £33.89 |
| Employee's NI at 10% 0f £135.55 | £13.56 |
| Employer's NI at 10.2% of £135.55 | £13.83 |
| Total due | £61.28 |

The organisation would have considerable unbudgeted costs, which may even push them into deficit.

Note that it is not enough to simply get a signed statement from someone to say that they are responsible for their own tax and national insurance. This may entitle you to sue the person concerned for any tax and national insurance you did have to pay to the Inland Revenue, but it does not remove your obligation to operate the PAYE system if the Inland Revenue consider that the person is an employee.

## Getting it right

You must be clear about the terms and conditions before you recruit someone; are you offering a contract for services or a contract of employment? There are fundamental differences from a legal aspect as well as the tax position. As the employer, you are entitled to decide that you want to employ all persons providing certain services. For example, you may decide as a matter of policy that all secretarial staff will be employees.

If you are in doubt about a particular position or a particular service, then it is wise to contact your inspector of taxes. It is best to put the details in writing to the inspector and obtain a written ruling. Telephone calls are not sufficient, and are not documented in the event of a query at some point in the future.

You should also be clear with consultants that they should be able to provide proof of their self-employed status. If they are newly self-employed, then they simply contact the nearest tax office (from the telephone directory) and a form will be sent to them so that they may register as self-employed. They may be eligible for the Enterprise Allowance Scheme, which offers free training to explain how to handle all these matters.

If someone is unwilling to co-operate and you still wish to use their services, then it is wise to withhold 25% tax from the gross due until they comply with your procedure.

## Trustees' Responsibilities

The trustees of charities have a duty to ensure that all funds are applied for charitable purposes. If the charity has to pay for additional liabilities due to incorrect procedures, this may be seen as an improper use of charitable assets. The trustees may be liable to make good the loss to the charity.

The trustees or management committee of unincorporated organisations are personally liable if the organisation has insufficient funds to meet its liabilities. The directors or management committee members of an incorporated charity may be personally liable if it can be shown that they acted negligently, disregarding professional advice given to them. Trustees should therefore ensure that there are proper procedures in place to deal with these matters.

Trustees should also draw up policy on the services which may be provided by self-employed consultants and review this from time to time. For example, they should consider whether they think it is appropriate for the chief executive of the organisation to be self-employed. What sort of contract should exist between the trustees and the chief executive?

If the trustees are satisfied that it is appropriate for the organisation to purchase services from consultants, then they should ensure that a standard contract is used for those personnel. It is wise to obtain the approval of a standard contract by a solicitor or accountant experienced in this area. An example is given here, but this does need to be adapted for the particular services and terms applying.

## Action Points – Self-Employed Personnel

**1.** Ensure that you are clear yourselves about whether you are offering a consultancy or an employment before you commence any recruitment.

**2.** Prepare written terms and conditions which should make the status of the work clear.

**3.** Check whether the person is VAT registered and will be providing a VAT invoice, as positive proof of self-employed status.

**4.** Make sure you receive an invoice from all self-employed personnel, even if not VAT registered. The invoice should look like the person is established in business, rather than something scribbled on the back of an envelope which does not even show their name and address.

**5.** Ask for their schedule D reference number. This is their tax district and file reference and will be some reassurance. (It should be in the format 123/12345.)

**6.** Write guidance notes for other people in the organisation who are likely to be responsible for appointing or hiring anyone on a self-employed basis.

**7.** Consult your inspector of taxes if you are unsure about someone's status or about the status of the work being offered.

**8.** Withhold 25% from the gross earnings if you do not receive adequate information, such as an invoice, from self- employed personnel. Alternatively, pay them the equivalent of net pay.

*Check Chapter 6 on volunteers also, to ensure that you do not unwittingly make volunteers your employees.*

---

**SAMPLE CONTRACT**

---

## The Promotion of the Arts Charity
## CONTRACT FOR SERVICES FOR CONSULTANTS

Name_____

Address_____

_____

_____ Tel_____

Schedule D reference number_____

VAT registered    Yes/No         Number_____

Description of the services:




The consultant undertakes to be punctual and professional in conduct at all times.

Confidentiality of personal information is required, and performance or behaviour to be discussed with the director only.


Date of supply_____

Fee £_____

Signed on behalf of The              Signed on behalf of the
Promotion of the Arts Charity        Consultant


_____    _____

_____ (date)       _____ (date)

# CASUAL LABOUR OR NOT ?

A popular misconception is that various categories of people working for you who are not full-time permanent employees may be classified as casual. In fact, the situations where payments may be made to anyone without deduction of tax are very few. So what is a casual employee?

A casual employee will be:

◆ employed by you

◆ taken on for one week or less

◆ not regularly employed by you

◆ someone who is not working for someone else

Casual employees are likely to be employed for the occasional session. They cannot be self-employed and a casual employee at the same time. Casual employees are not people like cleaners who only work for a few hours each week; that is regular employment, even though it is only part-time.

Even if you establish that the situation you are dealing with is such that it is casual employment, tax and national insurance may still need to be deducted. This will depend on the circumstances.

## Taxable Casual Employment

If you employ someone for one week or less, but their pay exceeds the weekly thresholds for tax and national insurance, then you must still deduct tax and national insurance from the pay. If the pay exceeds the national insurance threshold, but not the tax threshold, then only national insurance has to be deducted. No tax free pay should be given.

Even if their pay is below the threshold and you know that they also work for someone else, then you should also deduct tax and national insurance as appropriate. Ask them to complete a form P46, which asks them directly whether they have other employment.

## No Deductions

No deductions will need to be made if the amount payable to someone employed by you for one week or less is below the lower earnings limit for national insurance. You should still keep a record of their name, address and national insurance number. This may be needed at the end of the tax year for the completion of form P38A, Supplementary Return. This form has to be completed if you pay anyone £100 or more in a tax year without deducting tax and national insurance, even though these may have been genuine casual payments correctly made. The form asks for the employee's name, address, national insurance number and amount paid to them.

Since the computerisation of the PAYE system using national insurance numbers as the identification number, it will be possible for the Inland Revenue to pull together all the casual payments made to an individual. This might lead to a tax demand if they are due to pay more tax, although none may be due because they are entitled to the personal allowances, just the same as anyone else.

## Importance of good record keeping

It is the employer's responsibility to ensure that tax and national insurance is deducted when it should be. If you have made cash payments to anyone without making deductions, you need to be able to prove that you have acted in accordance with the rules. It is vital therefore that your records are in good order. A petty cash voucher for £50 with the narrative "casual payment" and an illegible signature scrawled on then bottom will not be sufficient. If you use casuals from time to time, then it is advisable that you devise a form for completion at the time the payment is made. This can be combined with some brief guidance notes to other staff in the organisation on the proper procedures.

## Penalties for non-compliance

A great number of charities have been faced with very large tax demands as a result of cash payments to employees without proper procedures. The demands are often the result of a routine inspection visit, when the inspectors will usually ask to see cash books and petty cash records, as well as payroll documents. If they find cash payments, then obviously they will look for proper back-up records. If you can provide all the information required, then there should be no problem. If, however, there are inadequate records, then some tax and national insurance could be due.

In the absence of evidence to the contrary, the Inland Revenue will assume that all cash payments should have had tax and national insurance deducted from them in full. So even if someone was a genuine casual, but you cannot show that, this may not help you. The calculation will assume that the amount you actually paid the person was the net pay and will work backwards from that.

### Example

You have paid someone £100 over two weeks and just gave them cash. You do not have their full name and address, nor national insurance number. You paid them out of your own pocket and reclaimed the amount on your own expenses.

£100 represents the net pay.

Tax at basic rate is 25% and employees have to contribute 10% in national insurance. In addition, the employer has to contribute 10.2% in national insurance.

So £100 is deemed to be after deduction of 25% tax and 10% national insurance – total deductions of 35%.

| Gross pay | 100% |
|-----------|------|
| Deductions | 35% |
| Net pay | 65% |

So £100 is the equivalent of 65% of gross pay and gross pay is therefore £153.85 (Calculate by £100 ÷ 65 x 100).

So Tax and NI due is:

| | | |
|---|---|---|
| tax @ 25% of £153.85 | = | £38.46 |
| employee's NI @ 10% of £153.85 | = | £15.39 |
| employer's NI @ 10.2% of £153.85 | = | £15.69 |
| Total tax and NI due | | £69.54 |

In addition to the extra bill for £69.54, you might also have to prove that the payment was not a taxable benefit to yourself, as it was paid to you as expenses!

As the example shows, the cost of mistakes in this area are very high. Cash payments made improperly can result in a tax demand for a further 69.54% of the cash originally paid out. This counters the argument that employing people through the payroll system costs the charity more money. In fact, it does not cost any more, but is likely to save the charity money. Inspection visits may not be very frequent, but when they visit, they are entitled to go back through the records for six years at least (longer if fraud is suspected). It is not uncommon for an assessment for tax on casual payments to make a calculation of tax and national insurance due for the most recent year, and then for this amount to be multiplied by six. The assumption is that you have been employing casuals at the same levels for six years. The onus is then on you, the employer, to prove that the demand is too high, or that cash payments were not made in the same way in earlier years, or whatever the true position is. This a costly and time-consuming exercise, which is avoided if the proper records are kept in the first place.

There is also a risk that the Inland Revenue will seek to charge interest on the late payment of tax and to levy penalties. Penalties will usually only be charged if the Inland Revenue consider that there was an attempt to deliberately defraud.

## Action Points – Casual Employees

**1.** Check that your organisation's procedures are clear about when casual employees may be used.

**2.** Ensure that everyone in the organisation understands that a casual employee can only be someone who works for one week or less.

**3.** Instigate proper forms that will comply with the requirements for record keeping.

**4.** Complete Supplementary Return P38A at the end of the tax year if anyone has been paid more than £100 without deductions.

**5.** Deduct tax and national insurance if you are paying them more than the tax threshold and put through the payroll as a temporary employee.

**6.** Make sure that cleaners and other part-time employees are on the payroll.

---

## SAMPLE FORM

---

**Community Care Charity**
**PAYMENTS TO CASUAL EMPLOYEES**

---

Surname of Employee:

Forenames:

Date of Birth:

Address:

National Insurance No.

---

Period of employment:                              Hours worked:

Nature of job:

Rate of pay applicable:

Total due:

Is the total due for the week more than £57?          Yes / No

Does this person have other work?          Yes / No

(If the answer to either question above is yes, then give them a form P46 and send this completed form to payroll)

Authorised_____(Manager)_____(date)

---

For Use in Finance:

Total paid:

Payroll?          Yes / No

Cost code:

                    Entered_____ Date_____

---

## SAMPLE GUIDANCE NOTES

**Community Care Charity**

**PAYMENTS TO CASUAL EMPLOYEES – GUIDANCE ON USE OF FORM**

Payments should only be made in cash where someone is undertaking sessional work and will be:

◆ working for one week or less
◆ paid less than £57 per week (for 1994/95 tax year) (£58 in 1995/96)
◆ the person does not work for anyone else

All sections of the form should be completed and signed by the manager. The form should then be passed to finance by the Monday following the week in which the payment was made.

Anyone working for other employers as well, taken on for more than one week or being paid more than £57 (£58) per week must be paid through payroll. The employee should be asked to complete a form P46. Managers should pass a blank form P46 to the employee and inform them that until the completed form is received by finance, they will not receive any pay.

Note that these forms are to be completed in addition to timesheets, but that timesheets also need to be received by finance promptly in order that the correct pay may be calculated.

---

# SPECIAL SITUATIONS

You may come across other situations where the person's status raises questions about how you should deal with payments to them.

## Multiple Employments

Employees who have more than one job will have to submit completed forms P46 when they start new jobs. The tax office will then collate all the information on that employee and instruct the employers on the tax code to use. National insurance is calculated in the same way as for other employees, although an employee who pays enough in one job may obtain exemption from paying further national insurance in other jobs. If they have not done this, they should be able to obtain a refund at the end of the tax year. They should ensure that their national insurance number is correctly quoted on their P60, so that all contributions are credited to their account.

## Agency Staff

If you use agency staff, then you have a contract with the agency, not with the individual. The individual is not your employee, but an employee of the agency. The agency is a business providing services and should issue you with an invoice. The invoice will probably bear VAT (making this a relatively expensive way of finding temporary staff for many charities, who may not be able to recover any of the VAT charged). You should deal with the invoice as you would for a purchase of any other goods or services.

Exceptionally, if you are asked to pay the agency worker direct or the agency is located overseas, then you should operate the PAYE system as for other employees.

## Students

There is a special concession available to students working in their holidays, which allows them to receive pay without deduction of tax. For this to apply, the student must:

◆ complete and sign form P38(S)

◆ be in full-time education

◆ have no other employment

◆ not have total taxable income in the tax year in excess of the personal allowance

◆ only work in the vacation period

The employer may then pay the student without deducting tax. If the earnings reach the lower earnings limit for national insurance contributions, then both employee's and employer's national insurance must be paid. You should set up a P11 (Deductions Working Sheet) for students as normal to keep a record of their pay. Keep the completed form P38(S) and send it in at the end of the tax year with the Employer's Summary (P35).

Students working during term-time should be treated as any other part-time employee. It is likely that you will have to deduct tax and national insurance, but follow the rules as usual (ask for P45 or get P46 completed).

If you regularly employ students, then a stock of leaflet IR60 from your tax office may be useful for handing out to students. This leaflet explains the basic rules to them.

## Pensioners

Pensioners have to pay tax on their taxable income, just as anyone else. The state pension they receive and any pension from a former employer is all taxable, as well as any interest on savings they may have. This means that they may well use up all their personal allowances to cover income from these sources and any earnings are fully taxable. It is not uncommon for pensioners to have a tax code of "BR" which means "basic rate". In other words all their earnings have to be taxed at basic rate of income tax. Great care should be exercised therefore, as even a few pounds earned each week is potentially taxable. If an employer takes on a pensioner, they should always send in the completed P46. Effectively, they do have another "job", which is their pension. Individual circumstances vary enormously and pensioners on low incomes and entitled to the higher rate of personal allowance (age allowance) may find that they do not have to pay a great deal of tax.

Pensioners do not have to make any more contributions to national insurance. An employer should use the "Employer Contributions Only" tables of the national insurance contribution tables. This currently applies to men over 65 years and women over 60 years. (The ages are gradually being changed as the pension ages are being equalised.) Note also that Statutory Sick Pay does not apply to those over 65 years in age.

If you are paying pensions to retired employees, then they should be paid as employees. Frequently, however, a separate trust is actually paying the pensions, so the trust will be responsible for administration and the operation of PAYE.

## Workers Abroad

Many charities send their employees to work overseas. Anyone staying outside the UK for more than 365 days can claim a 100% deduction from paying tax. This period does not have to coincide with the tax year and it means that tax does not have to be paid on those earnings. There are rules limiting the visits to the UK:

◆ the total of days in the UK may not exceed a maximum of one-sixth of period

◆ maximum of 62 days in UK

Care must be taken with the interpretation of these rules, especially the rule about one-sixth of the overseas period. If the absence qualifies for the 100% deduction, then it should not matter where the pay is remitted and it is quite normal for pay to be credited to UK bank accounts. The individual does not lose UK residence in these circumstances and may still claim personal allowances, MIRAS relief and other reliefs. Their other income is still taxable.

This will not be the case if an individual is absent for a whole tax year, as then they become non-resident. Non-residents do not receive personal allowances, anf generally their income is not taxable.

Workers abroad need to consider their position from the point of view of national insurance. They may well be advised to pay voluntary contributions (Class 3) to retain their pension rights. This class of contributions will not give them entitlement to Statutory Sick Pay, Statutory Maternity Pay, unemployment benefit and a number of other benefits.

Employees working overseas for shorter periods will usually pay tax on all their earnings and should be paid as usual through the PAYE system.

This is a complex area and you may well need to check your position before taking action.

## Young Employees

Employees under 16 do not have to pay national insurance contributions. They are entitled to their own personal allowance and so are unlikely to pay tax, although it will depend on the level of their income.

## Trainees

Trainees under government sponsored schemes or on other full-time training schemes are not usually employees. They may be paid trainee allowances within certain limits, travel allowances and an allowance for sick pay without any tax liability arising. They may also receive benefits such as free places in a nursery for their child or children without tax implications. As long as the allowances are within agreed guidelines, these will not affect the individual's claims to most benefits, but this may depend on their personal circumstances.

If someone is receiving 'on-the-job' training and working at the same time, then they are an employee. They are usually paid a salary which is subject to tax and national insurance as usual.

Specific arrangements for particular trades and professions sometimes exist and information is usually available from the trade association or relevant professional body.

Students on 'sandwich' courses will have to pay tax and national insurance on salaries they earn during periods of employment.

## Seconded staff

Companies may second staff to charities as a tax effective way of giving to the charity. The company keeps the staff on their payroll, as they are still the employees of the company. Agreement would have to be reached about such matters as expenses, which the charity may reimburse to the employee. These would have to be reported to the company, in order that they may complete the end of year documentation such as form P11D.

### Action Points – Employees in special situations

**1.** Check that employees with more than one job have completed a P46, that it has been sent to your tax office and keep a copy with their P11 or personnel records.

**2.** Check contracts for agency staff. Investigate cheaper alternatives, such as casual staff on your own short-term contract.

**3.** Check that you are using the P38(S) for holiday jobs for students.

**4.** Check that you have details of the age of employees. Those over pension age do not pay national insurance, but are not eligible for SSP.

**5.** Check on visits to UK employees working abroad for at least a year.

# Chapter 3

# WHAT COUNTS AS PAY ?

This chapter looks at cash payments to employees and the taxable or non-taxable status of them. Expenses payments are dealt with more extensively in the chapter on benefits. There is also a separate chapter on national insurance which explains the concept of earnings and when national insurance contributions have to be made.

## Taxable Pay

As a general principle all amounts paid to employees are assumed to be part of their contract and taxable. A payment for work done or an inducement to work better should all be included in taxable pay. Usually such amounts should be included in gross pay for tax purposes. Obviously, you must tax salary or wages. Taxable pay will also include:

◆ overtime

◆ payments for additional duties e.g. sleep in payments

◆ bonuses or commission

◆ Statutory Sick Pay

◆ Statutory Maternity Pay

◆ additional sick leave or maternity leave payments

◆ holiday pay

◆ back pay

◆ pensions to former employees

◆ round sum allowances

In some cases no tax will actually be payable. For example, the maternity pay due to someone may be less than the personal allowance due to them according to their tax code. So an individual's personal circumstances will determine how much tax they pay.

## Non Taxable Payments

As a general rule, payments which are not made as a contractual obligation are not taxable. Some of the situations where these may arise are discussed in more depth below. Some situations where payments are not taxable:

◆ student grants (full-time education)

◆ trainee allowances (full-time courses)

◆ grants to individuals in need

## Cash Allowances

Allowances paid to employees should be assumed taxable, unless you have agreement from the tax office to the contrary. This includes such cash sums as meals allowances for working abnormal hours. Note that the provision of a meal would not necessarily be taxable, but the cash allowance is taxable pay. The employee may be able to claim a deduction for costs incurred in carrying out their duties. It should be remembered here that the costs would have to be "wholly, exclusively and necessarily" incurred in the performance of their duties. The difficulty here is that the courts have decided in numerous cases to interpret this quite strictly. "A person eats to live, not to work."

Note that the provision of meals in certain circumstances, protective clothing, uniforms and certain other items will not usually be taxable, but the provision of an allowance in lieu is taxable. The reimbursement of a business expense will not be taxable, although it may have to be declared and a deduction claimed.

## Round Sum Allowances

Round sum allowances are taxable, even if they are intended for expenditure on travel etc. required for the performance of the employee's duties. The employer would be required to add the round sum allowance to the gross pay and tax and national insurance has to be calculated in the normal way. The employee could claim the actual amount spent on business expenses on their tax return as a deduction. They would receive the tax relief as an adjustment to their tax code or as a refund after an assessment has been issued. The employee and employer would still have paid the national insurance, however, on the round sum allowance. It is more tax efficient to operate a system of reimbursing employees for expenses actually incurred, upon submission of an expenses claim form. Guidelines could be given to employees on the level of expenses they should be claiming if you wished to limit these. The expenses claim forms would have to be approved before payment was made as a further control.

Allowances paid to employees because of the terms and conditions of employment are all taxable. For example, an employee may be paid an allowance for working unsocial hours or because they are required to work in different locations. These all amount to remuneration in one form or another and are probably just a way of calculating different scales of pay for different employees. They should be included in the gross pay and tax and national insurance calculated as normal.

## Essential Car User Allowance

Many charity employees are paid according to the scales and terms used by local authorities. Essential car user allowances are paid to certain employees who have to use their own car in their job. This allowance is usually in addition to a mileage rate. These allowances are taxable, since they are a round sum allowance. You may be able to put a case to the local tax office for certain employees with low mileage and obtain their agreement that the allowance need not be treated as gross pay. They will look at the particular circumstances, including the amount of the round sum allowance, the mileage rates paid and the average business miles. If the rate overall is no more than the tax allowable rates under the Fixed Profit Car Scheme, then it may be agreed that the allowance may be paid tax-free. This can get complicated, though, so consider whether, in fact, mileage can simply be reimbursed.

## Expense Floats

The employee may be advanced a float for expenses, if the trustees wish to keep down the frequency of expense claims and the expenses incurred are quite high. For example, a fundraiser may work from home using their own telephone and car, and carrying costs until they make an expenses claim monthly. A reasonable level of float may be advanced to the employee without this being a taxable payment. The float should be properly documented and the employee should sign a form to indicate that they have received the money and that they understand that it will have to be repaid. It is usual for the float to be recovered from the last month's net pay when the employee leaves. It may be wise to ensure that the amount of the float is not excessive, and certainly not more than one month's net pay. Otherwise it may be difficult to recover the float.

Note that expense claims should be submitted and paid just the same, even if an employee has a float.

## Ex-Gratia Payments

Most commonly, the situation arises when an employee leaves. It is possible to make a payment to a former employee which is non- taxable, providing it is not a payment for work done. Nor should it be "custom and practice" to make such payments. If an employee has a reasonable expectation that they will receive such a payment, then it could be an implied contract term and all contractual payments are taxable. The ex-gratia payment should not be holiday pay or related in any way to past service. In effect, it has to be a gift, which may be for that individual's personal qualities, but not a reward in any other sense.

For charities, there is a particular problem in making an ex- gratia payment, since it is not evident that this is a payment in furtherance of the charity's objects, and trustees must always act in the best interests of the beneficiaries of the charity at all times. Charity trustees need to exercise great care in this area. They must feel justified in making such a gift, but it may be difficult to demonstrate that an ex-gratia payment is furthering the charity's objects. However, trustees may feel a moral obligation to make such a payment, over and beyond their contractual obligations. In this situation, they must go to the Charity Commissioners and request permission to make the payment. Prior to the 1992 Charities Act, trustees had to obtain the authority of the court, not just the Charity Commission, which could take some time. Clearly this is a measure to protect the assets of the charity and to ensure that they are properly applied to the charitable objects. Small ex-gratia payments are unlikely to cause a problem, but advice nonetheless must be sought from the Charity Commission.

## Lump Sums on Retirement

Substantial ex-gratia payments to employees upon their retirement are unlikely to be true ex-gratia payments. Such payments are taxable in full as they are considered to be part of a package of benefits due on retirement. You will probably need to get advice from your Inland Revenue office, as the amounts involved may be substantial. The situation may also be complicated where there is a mixed motive for the payment, such as compensation for loss of office. This aspect is dealt with in more detail under the section on Redundancy payments below.

## Honoraria

Honoraria are really another form of payment for work. Usually they are called honoraria because they are not commensurate with the amount of work actually involved and are really just a small recognition. They are often paid to voluntary officers of a charity, or sometimes to employees for extra duties not in their contract. Despite the fact that they are often small, honoraria will nearly always be taxable, in principle. Where an honorarium is paid to an employee, it should be added to their gross pay and taxed through the PAYE system as normal.

The treatment of honoraria to other individuals will have to follow the normal PAYE rules and will depend on their particular circumstances. You need to consider whether the person has other taxable income, whether it is a one-off payment and whether they are self-employed. Follow the guidance on Card 5 of the Employer's Basic Guide to PAYE (P8) and check Chapter 2 on whether they are an employee. The following practical examples may also help you to identify the appropriate course of action.

### Example 1

A series of talks have been organised by your charity and speakers from the academic world invited to speak. It has been agreed to offer speakers an honorarium of £50 as well as travel expenses.

The honorarium is a taxable payment. The speaker is being employed for one session and therefore is similar to a casual employee. The amount being paid is less than the tax and national insurance thresholds and therefore you only need to keep a record of their name and address. Alternatively, you could see them as self-employed, because you are offering a fixed fee for a talk. For a small fee, a signed form or receipt would be sufficient documentation.

## Example 2

Jamal is secretary of the local scout group. He has used his own computer and spent a great deal of time on the affairs of the group. The executive committee vote to pay him an honorarium of £100 as a gesture of thanks for all his work and to cover some of his expenses in the use of the computer and stationery.

Since Jamal does have a job, tax at basic rate and national insurance should be deducted from the payment. If he is reimbursed for the expenses only, then this would not be taxable, providing he could produce receipts and evidence to support the claim.

## Payments by Third Parties

An employee may receive a fee for giving a talk or an appearance on television. If the fee is paid to the employee direct, then it is up to them to declare the income on their tax return. They will receive an assessment and pay tax if necessary.

If the fee is paid to the charity, then this is income to the charity and will not usually affect the employee's pay at all. If the charity decides to pass on the fee to the employee, then it is taxable pay, must be added to the gross pay for the month and tax and national insurance calculated as normal.

The charity may need a policy on such matters, so that the right to receive such fees is clear. The trustees may feel that the employee has gained knowledge and experience through their paid work for the charity and that consequently all fees should come to the charity. On the other hand, if an employee writes a book in their own time and earns a fee and royalties, then it might be considered that this is outside their duties as charity employee. The employee would be entitled to receive the fee and royalties as their own income. They would have to declare the income to the Inland Revenue on their tax return. If they do not automatically receive a tax return, then they should request one from the tax office dealing with the payroll for their main employment.

Care may be needed if non-cash benefits are provided by a third party instead of pay. These would have to be declared by the employer at the year end. This is covered in more detail in the chapter on benefits.

## Redundancy Pay

The term redundancy pay is often used quite loosely to cover payments in various situations where employment is terminated. To establish the tax position, we will need to distinguish between the different types of termination payments.

A basic principle is that contractual payments are taxable, whereas non-contractual payments are not taxable. If the contract of employment specifies the entitlement to payment in certain situations then this will be taxable.

Statutory redundancy pay is not taxable and not subject to national insurance. The conditions and amounts of statutory redundancy pay are set out in the Employment Protection (Consolidation) Act 1978 and subsequent statutory instruments varying the rates. The broad outline of the legislation is that continuous employment is required for full-time employees for two years before any redundancy becomes payable. The basic entitlement is then one week's pay for every year of service, although this rate is higher for older employees. A maximum of 20 years' service can be counted and there is a maximum weekly pay set from time to time.

Employers will often seek to enhance the redundancy terms. If the non-statutory redundancy pay is included in the contract of employment or it has become custom and practice to make such payments such that employees have a right to expect the payment, then these will be taxable in full. However, the Inland Revenue will accept that the first £30,000 of such payments may be exempt from tax if the redundancy is genuine and not an award for past service. To demonstrate that the scheme is a genuine redundancy scheme, the employer should:

♦ be operating the scheme only in cases of redundancy as defined in the Employment Protection (Consolidation) Act 1978

♦ only pay redundancy where the individual has at least two years' continuous service

♦ be paying all redundant employees under the scheme, not just a selected few

♦ ensure that the payments are not excessively large in relation to earnings and length of service

Before any payments are made in such circumstances, it is wise to obtain the agreement of the local inspector of taxes that the first £30,000 may be paid tax-free. A retrospective inspection which identified that these were subject to tax in full would mean an extra liability for the employer.

The tax-free band of £30,000 will also apply to various other termination payments. Generally, a payment in compensation for loss of office will be eligible for the tax-free band, but great care should be exercised, as a contractual or expected payment is fully taxable. A lump sum payment to a retiring employee will be fully taxable if it is seen as part of the benefit package on retirement and not part of an approved scheme. Payments to permanently disabled employees or in situations where employment is terminated due to long term sickness will qualify for the tax- free band of £30,000

Note that charities making ex-gratia payments in these circumstances need to obtain the approval of the Charity Commission and be prepared to show that there is a strong moral obligation to make the payment.

## Payment in Lieu of Notice

By its nature, a payment to an employee working out a period of notice is a contractual payment and therefore taxable. Where the employee is not required to work out their period of notice, then the employer is, in effect, in breach of contract. Payment in lieu of notice is then a damages payment to compensate the employee for the loss and may be made without deduction of tax or national insurance. This does not apply to accrued holiday pay, overtime or bonuses due, which would have to be paid through the PAYE system as normal. If the contract of employment states that the notice entitlement may be paid as a lump sum instead of being worked, then this becomes a contractual payment and as such subject to normal PAYE.

## Payments after Termination

There will be situations where the employee is entitled to pay after they have left your employment and after you have provided the leaving certificate (P45). Commonly a backdated pay increase is awarded and should be paid to former employees as well as current employees. In these circumstances, the payment should be made after deduction of basic rate tax (using code BR on Pay Adjustment Tables) and national insurance.

### Action Points – Payments and Allowances

**1.** Ensure that all cash payments such as overtime and payments for extra duties are included in gross pay.

**2.** Avoid paying cash allowances for meals, clothing etc. Pay for such expenses direct or reimburse the actual cost through an expense claim.

**3.** Avoid round sum allowances for things such as car usage or overnight stays. Reimburse the actual cost.

**4.** Do not make regular ex-gratia payments, as these then become custom and practice and therefore taxable.

**5.** Do not try to convert holiday pay, overtime due, etc. into an ex-gratia payment when someone leaves.

**6.** Instead of paying honoraria, pay expenses. You may make a gift, but this should be a pure gift not a disguised payment for work done. For visiting speakers, you might offer them a gift to the charity of their choice.

**7.** If you have to make staff redundant, check the scheme with the Inland Revenue before making any payments to staff.

# Chapter 4
# BENEFITS

Complicated rules have been created over the years to bring non- cash payments to directors and employees within the scope of tax. Benefits in kind are an obvious method of attempting to remunerate staff without tax applying, but many of the loopholes have been closed. Both tax and national insurance will apply to many of the benefits provided to employees.

## Return of Employee's Expenses Payments and Benefits

Employers must be aware of the rules and are obliged to declare any benefits provided at the end of the tax year on a form P11D or form P9D. Note that you should still include expenses payments and benefits, even if these are provided by a third party. Similarly, you have to include benefits provided to the employee or any members of that person's family. These forms will usually sent to you automatically, but you should request them if you do not receive them.

- ◆ **Form P11D** – to be completed for company directors and employees earning at a rate of £8,500 per annum or more.

- ◆ **Form P9D** – to be completed for employees earning at a rate of less than £8,500 per annum if they receive any taxable benefits.

- ◆ **Form P11D(b)** – a certificate to be completed by the employer confirming that all necessary forms P11D and P9D have been completed and submitted.

The threshold of £8,500 has been the same for a great number of years and used to be the amount above which an employee was considered to be higher paid. Although this is clearly no longer the case, the distinction is still made.

Charities will need to consider the use of form P9D for caretakers and wardens, for example, when you need to look carefully to check whether any of the benefits are taxable or not. The form need only be completed where taxable benefits are provided which have not been included in gross pay on the Deductions Working Sheet P11. The reimbursement of expenses need not be counted or disclosed on the P9D, although round sum allowances would need to be shown.

Most employers will be completing P11D's for the majority of their staff. You must still include part-time staff if their rate of pay is more than £8,500 per annum for the full-time equivalent, and also include staff who have only worked for part of the year, but earn at a rate of more than £8,500 per annum. This threshold includes expenses payments and the value of any benefits as well as salary. It is likely to include the majority of employees.

P11D's should also be completed and submitted for all company directors, but the directors of charities are specifically excluded, providing they receive less than £8,500 in remuneration, expenses payments and benefits. This will therefore exclude most trustees, committee members, directors and members of governing bodies. A P11D may be required, however, if trustees undertake a great deal of international travel. Expenses payments do count towards the £8,500 threshold, even if they are a reimbursement of actual expenses.

It is important to submit P11D's for all directors and employees to whom they apply because the penalties for non-compliance are severe. The employer is responsible for making the return and failure to do within the time limit results in a penalty of up to £300 for each missing return, with a further penalty of up to £60 per day for continuing failure to submit the return. Returns should be sent in by 6 June each year. The penalty for incorrect returns is a maximum of £3,000 per return.

## Dispensations

Clearly, a lot of work is involved for employers at the end of the tax year when they have to complete P11D's for all their staff. Note that the form requires details of all expenses payments as well as taxable benefits. It therefore includes expenses payments which are simply a reimbursement of the costs incurred by the employee in the course of carrying out their duties for the employer. The employee would then have to submit a claim with their tax return that they have spent an equivalent amount on costs which were wholly, exclusively and necessarily incurred in the course of performing their duties.

Where this is the case, the inspector of taxes may agree to a dispensation so that the reimbursement of expenses do not have to be shown on P11D's. Typically, dispensations are granted for the reimbursement of travel and subsistence costs to employees. The employer will need to show that there is a proper system within the organisation for checking the validity of expense claims. A dispensation will not be granted for the payment of round sum allowances. The dispensation may exclude the most senior management if there is no mechanism for checking their expenses, although the structure of charities usually allows for the treasurer to review the expenses of senior staff.

Employers apply for a dispensation by writing to the local inspector of taxes setting out:

◆ the type of expenses to which the dispensation will apply

◆ the categories of employees to whom the dispensation will apply

◆ the system of control over expenses payments

Once obtained, the dispensation removes the need for those expenses to be entered on a P11D or for the employee to claim for the expenses to be allowed as tax deductible on their tax return. The P11D will still need to be completed for those employees where they receive other benefits. It is important to retain the letter from the inspector of taxes granting the dispensation, also known as a notice of nil liability.

# NON-TAXABLE PAYMENTS AND BENEFITS

There are some benefits which are not taxable and it may be useful to bear these in mind when planning an overall remuneration package.

## Pension Plans

Contributions by an employer to an approved pension plan or provision of a pension after retirement through an approved employer's scheme are not taxable. Generally, there is no limit on the tax relief for employer's contributions.

## Training

Employees undergoing training at the employer's expense are not taxed on the benefit they receive. Driving lessons at the employer's expense are included, but the training should be necessary for the employee's job. This would be required under charity law also, as a charity may only apply its assets and income to charitable purposes.

## Travel and Subsistence

Where employees incur costs in the course of carrying out their duties, they are entitled to recover the costs from their employer without suffering tax. Proper records should be maintained to show that the employee is only being reimbursed for the actual costs they incurred. Any profit element will be taxable, as will flat rate allowances. Mileage allowances and the provision of cars and fuel are special situations considered below.

Employers may pay for disabled persons to travel between home and work without a taxable benefit arising; they may also pay for transport home for employees required to work late occasionally. Transport may also be provided when public transport is disrupted due to industrial action.

Employees who carry out their duties abroad may be reimbursed for the cost of travel to their place of work, or the costs may be paid direct by the employer. This may also include members of the employee's family.

## Relocation Expenses

Employers may pay a relocation package to a new employee or to an employee who is being asked to move because of a change in their duties. The move should be permanent and should mean that the employee's main residence changes. The move has to be to bring the employee within "reasonable daily travelling distance" of their normal place of work. The total amount which may be paid tax-free is limited to £8,000 Any amounts paid over the limit should be declared on the P11D at the end of the tax year.

The package may include payments for the following:

◆ costs of selling their old home (e.g. legal fees, estate agent's fees, etc.)

◆ costs of buying the new home (e.g. stamp duty)

◆ any abortive costs on buying a new home if a purchase falls through for reasons beyond the control of the employee

◆ removal costs, including storage and insurance

◆ travel and subsistence costs while employee and family are travelling to the new area to find accommodation, organise the move and any transitional period

◆ cost of a bridging loan

◆ duplicate expenses, being the net expenses of replacing domestic goods not suitable in the new home (e.g. a fridge freezer that does not fit into the new kitchen)

## Lunch or Canteen Facilities

An employer may provide a canteen for staff without this being a taxable benefit. The food and drink may be provided free or at a subsidised rate. It must, however, be available to all employees, not just the directors or senior staff of the organisation. If the employee is required to work away from the normal place of work, then they will be entitled to claim for the cost of lunches (or applicable meals) if they would have received these in the canteen otherwise. The employer may set an upper limit for such claims, but the employee should not simply claim a flat rate allowance.

Staff who receive free meals while they are on duty are not taxed on this benefit. This would apply to staff working in residential care homes, who eat with the residents as part of their duties.

## Luncheon Vouchers

Employees may be given luncheon vouchers to a maximum value of 15p per day. Vouchers given above this amount must be taxed.

## Workplace Nurseries

Employees who receive free or subsidised places in a workplace nursery are not taxed on the benefit (since 1990). This does not apply to other forms of childcare, however, and an employee receiving a contribution from an employer for childminder fees or other forms of childcare is taxed on the benefit. It does not have to be full-time and the employer could be providing the childcare as part of a consortium. So a group of organisations could arrange for childcare in the school holidays. Note that the childcare provision may not be in someone's home and it should be registered under the Nurseries and Child-Minders Regulation Act 1948 or the Children Act 1989.

## Accommodation

If it is part of someone's job that they have to live in accommodation provided by the employer, then this will not be a taxable benefit. This will usually apply to residential wardens in sheltered housing schemes, caretakers and other similar positions. It should be necessary for the proper performance of the employee's duties that they reside in the accommodation or the accommodation is provided for the better performance of the employee's duties and the employment is one of the kinds for which it is customary for accommodation to be provided.

In the situations described above, there may be a taxable benefit on expenses borne by the employer, such as lighting, heating, cleaning, repairs, maintenance, decoration, provision of furniture etc. The taxable benefit will be limited to 10% of the gross pay for tax purposes (after deduction of superannuation or pension contributions by the employee), less any sum made good by the employee.

No taxable benefit will arise if a housing association provides accommodation to an employee or management committee member on terms compatible with the normal terms offered to all other tenants.

## Car Parking

The provision of a car parking space at or near the employee's place of work is not a taxable benefit.

## Gifts and Entertainment

Long service awards are not benefits, as long as they are not in the form of cash or a form which may be converted into cash. A gift may be of reasonable cost, which is no more than £20 per year of service.

Gifts for Christmas, birthdays, weddings, etc. will not be taxable if they are given to the employee in a personal capacity and not as a reward for work done.

Gifts from third parties up to a limit of £100 per tax year are permitted and entertainment from a third party is also allowed. It may not be a person connected to the employer, nor the employer. Presumably, the most likely source of such gifts and entertaining are suppliers or potential suppliers. Your organisation may have its own code of practice about the acceptance of gifts by employees for reasons other than taxation.

The employer may provide a party or other entertainment for employees once a year, where the cost per head does not exceed £50 as a non-taxable benefit. This applies to Christmas parties or other such events.

## Medical Expenses

Employers may pay for medical insurance or medical treatment for employees working overseas, providing the need for the medical attention arises while they are overseas performing their duties. In other situations, this would be a taxable benfit.

## Medical Check-Ups

An employer may provide routine health checks or medical screening without a taxable benefit arising. The checks may be provided in-house if the organisation has its own medical staff or by an outside firm.

## Sporting and Recreational Facilities

The provision of sporting or recreational facilities is not a taxable benefit. The facility should be available generally to all employees and may be extended to members of their families. The facility may be provided by way of vouchers, as long as these cannot be exchanged for cash. Facilities not included, however, are holiday homes, hotel accommodation, motor racing, boats, aircraft and various other recreational facilities! It is intended to allow organisations to set sports clubs which may have a bar etc. without a taxable benefit arising for every employee.

## TAXABLE BENEFITS

Any payment to an employee is potentially taxable. Even the reimbursement of expenses could be liable to tax, unless the expenses were incurred wholly and exclusively in the course of the performance of duties. Unless you have a dispensation, then the total of the expenses payments to all employees earning at a rate of £8,500 per annum must be shown on the P11D. The employee then needs to complete the relevant section on his or her tax return to claim these as business expenses.

## Flat Rate Allowances

Generally a flat rate allowance will be seen as another form of payment for work and therefore taxable. If you pay an allowance for the use of employees' own cars, for example, this should normally be added to gross pay on the P11 (Deductions Working Sheet). Tax and national insurance will therefore be calculated in the normal way on these payments and there is no need to include them on the P11D.

## Travel Between Home and Work

If the employer pays for the cost of travel between home and the normal place of work, then this will be taxable. For example, the provision of a season ticket to an employee would have to be taxed as a benefit. The "normal place of work" is where the employee spends 50% of their time. Employees who do not have a "normal place of work" need to take care; they should only claim for travel expenses once they start their work. The rule is that the employees are responsible for getting themselves into a position to commence their work.

Employees who are required to attend work outside normal working hours may receive the cost of their travel between home and work tax free. For example, an employee required to stay late for an evening meeting may require a taxi home for reasons of safety or lack of public transport. This would not be a taxable benefit as long as it was an irregular occurrence. If, however, the nature of the employment was such that shift hours were part of the job and inevitably meant travel at unsocial hours, then the normal rules applying to travel between home and work would apply. If the employer paid for the travel, it would be a taxable benefit.

Disabled persons receiving assistance with the cost of travel between home and work are not receiving a taxable benefit.

## Interest-Free Loans

Frequently, employers lend the cost of an annual season ticket to employees, or perhaps a loan is made for the purchase of a car where this is required for the performance of duties. (Note that charities should not be making loans to employees unless the trustees can demonstrate that the loan is fulfilling a charitable purpose, so guidelines should be fairly restrictive on the purpose for which loans are given to staff.)

From 1994/95 there is a de minimis limit, such that loans of amounts of £5,000 or less are ignored altogether. Notional interest is calculated at a rate set by the Inland Revenue from time to time on loans for larger amounts and this amount is the taxable benefit. This should be shown on the P11D for the employee.

## Private Health Insurance

This is insurance for private medical care in the event of illness. If the employer pays the premiums on this type of insurance, then it will be a taxable benefit on the employee and must be shown on the P11D. There are certain exceptions for people over the age of 60 years and those working abroad.

## "In-House" Benefits – basis of valuation

Employees often receive benefits because of the particular trade in which they are employed. These do have to be declared as taxable benefits, but the basis on which they should be valued can cause long negotiation with the Inland Revenue. A case which went all the way to the House of Lords (Pepper v. Hart) has recently set a new precedent for the valuation basis. The case concerned the provision of free places in a fee-paying school to the children of teachers in the school. The Inland Revenue had been arguing that the benefit was the *average* cost to the employer of a place in the school. The House of Lords finally decided that the value of the benefit was the *extra* cost to the school of providing the free place. This basis of valuation will now apply to all "in-house" benefits.

It is accepted that no additional benefit arises where teachers pay 15% or more of normal school fees.

In other cases, no taxable benefit arises if the employee pays at least the wholesale price of goods, or where professional services are provided without incurring additional staff costs.

## Mobile Telephones

A flat rate taxable benefit of £200 applies to mobile and car telephones. This is for the private use of the telephone, so if the employee does not use the telephone for private calls or they reimburse the employer for the full cost of private calls, then no taxable benefit arises. Note that the Inland Revenue would expect the employee to make a contribution towards the original cost of the telephone as well as the direct cost of the calls. An amount of 20% of the original market value is considered acceptable, but if the telephone is primarily used for business calls, then there is no need for the employee to pay a proportion of the line rental, as this cost would be incurred by the employer anyway. (This is the accepted practice since the decision in the Pepper v. Hart case November 1992.)

## Vouchers

Vouchers provided by the employer to employees are taxable benefits and must be included in the P11D. Vouchers which cannot be converted into cash need to be entered on the P11D on the basis of the cost to the employer. Vouchers which can be exchanged for cash should be valued at the exchange value.

## SPECIAL SITUATIONS

There are a few situations where the tax treatment is fairly complicated and the taxable or non-taxable nature of the expense or benefit will depend on the circumstances. There have also been considerable changes to some of the legislation in this area.

## Cars

Frequently the employer will buy or lease cars for the use of employees who regularly travel a great deal as part of their work. It will always be assumed that the employee receives some benefit from the provision of the car, even if private use of the car is minimal. Just the use of the car for travel between home and work is private use and a taxable benefit. It is also assumed that the employer pays for all the costs such as insurance, tax, repairs, breakdown service, business fuel. (See below for the tax consequences of providing fuel for private mileage.)

The rate at which the benefit is taxed does not reflect the varying amount of private use and the varying levels of benefit received by different employees to that extent. Up until 5 April 1994, the taxable benefit to an employee of a car was based on a scale charge. Each year the Inland Revenue would publish tables which showed the deemed taxable benefit to an employee for various categories of vehicle. The categories depended on the age and power of the car. So, for example, the scale charge for a three year old Ford Escort 1300 for the tax year 1993/94 is £3,465 where the business miles are less than 2,500 per year. This would be adjusted on the employee's tax code such that the code is reduced, the amount of tax free pay reduced and the tax on the benefit collected month by month through PAYE deductions. Any contribution by the employee towards private use would be deducted from the scale charge. For 1994/95 tax year the system has changed. The scale rates will no longer be used, but the taxable benefit will be assessed at 35% of the list price of the car when originally purchased. Further adjustments to this valuation of the benefit will be made as follows:

| | |
|---|---|
| High business miles: | |
| 2,500 – 18,000 per year | reduce value by one third |
| more than 18,000 per year | reduce value by two thirds |
| Older cars: | |
| more than 4 years at end of tax year | reduce value by a further one third |
| Car available for part of tax year | reduce value by proportion of year not available |
| Contributions by employee | reduce value by the amount contributed |

The list price of a car is the price published by the manufacturer or distributor on the day before the car was first registered. It includes charges such as delivery, taxes, extras. Additional accessories fitted at a later date costing more than £100 (including VAT) also have to be included in the list price. A publisher has produced a guide to all the list prices for several years, but unfortunately the book costs approximately £105, which is probably not worthwhile for most employers where there are only a few cars. You may ask your local tax office to look up the list price for you in order that you may calculate the benefit.

Note that national insurance contributions are also payable by the employer on car benefits.

## Pool Cars

Where a car is shared between many users, then it may qualify as a pool car and there is no taxable benefit to any of the users. To qualify as a pool car, the following conditions must apply:

◆ the car must be used by more than one employee

◆ the car should be a pool car for the tax year

◆ the car should not usually be taken home at night by an employee

◆ the car should be used principally for business trips

It will be acceptable for an employee to take the car home one evening so that they can make an early start the next morning. This should be the exception rather than a regular occurrence.

The Inland Revenue come down very hard on artificial claims that a vehicle is a pool car. They may make every driver of the vehicle liable for a taxable benefit, so that the one vehicle gives rise to several tax bills. This will certainly not be welcomed by the employees who pay the tax!

## Pool Vans

Your organisation may have a van or minibus, which may well have the organisation's name emblazoned on the side. Private use of such a vehicle is still a taxable benefit, although the tax charge is less than the rates for cars. Remember that private use will include travel between home and work on a regular basis. The taxable benefit arises if the vehicle is available for private use, rather than just on the actual private use. The taxable benefit is a flat rate of £500 (reduced to £350 if the vehicle is more than four years old), which may be shared between several employees if they all have access to the vehicle for private use.

## Fuel for Private Use

If the employer pays for all the fuel, then there is also a taxable benefit of fuel provided for private mileage. The taxable value of the benefit is calculated according to a table of scale charges, similar to the old system for car benefits. So the employee with the Ford Escort 1300 who claims all their petrol bills from their employer will also have to pay tax on a fuel scale charge of £640 in 1994/95. Note that these scale charges will still be the system for taxing fuel benefit after 6 April 1994; it is only the car scale charges which have been changed.

If the employee pays for all their petrol for private use, then no fuel scale charge arises.

Note that national insurance contributions are also payable on fuel benefit using the same scale rates.

| Car Fuel Scale Rates | 1994/95 | | 1995/96 | |
|---|---|---|---|---|
| Size of Car | Petrol | Diesel | Petrol | Diesel |
| Up to 1,400 cc | £640 | £580 | £670 | £605 |
| 1,401 cc to 2,000 cc | £810 | £580 | £850 | £605 |
| 2,001 cc or more | £1,200 | £750 | £1260 | £780 |
| Without a cc | £1,200 | | £1260 | |

## Mileage Allowances

If employees use their own cars for work, then it is usual to reimburse for the cost by paying a mileage rate. The rate is designed to cover the petrol cost, but also a proportion of the capital cost, the insurance, repairs, etc. This is a potential problem as the tax rules are that an expense is only tax deductible if it has been incurred "wholly, exclusively and necessarily" for the business or trade. As a concession, the condition of exclusivity is suspended for mileage allowances.

Nonetheless, the Inland Revenue will collect tax on mileage rates which do more than simply reimburse the cost. The Inland Revenue set out tax-free rates in tables each year. If employers agree to pay only these rates, then they may join the Fixed Profit Car Scheme and no taxable benefit arises. If the employer pays mileage allowances at rates higher than the rates in the tables, then a taxable benefit arises on the excess or "profit" being made by the employee.

If you wish to obtain a dispensation from completing P11D's for employees claiming mileage allowances, then you will have to use the non-profit rates in the Fixed Profit Car Scheme.

**The non-profit rates in 1994/95 are:**

|  | to 4,000 miles in year | over 4,000 miles in year |
|---|---|---|
| Up to 1,000 cc | 27p | 15p |
| 1,001-1,500 cc | 33p | 19p |
| 1,501-2,000 cc | 41p | 23p |
| Over 2,000 cc | 56p | 31p |

The Fixed Profit Car Scheme rates for 1995/96 are published in March 1995 and are available from your local Inspector of Taxes.

**Action Points – Benefits and Expenses**

**1.** Obtain a dispensation for travel and subsistence expenses for all employees if possible.

**2.** Ensure that expenses are claimed on proper expense claims and authorised by an appropriate person.

**3.** Ensure that adequate records are kept for taxable benefits.

**4.** Establish a recording system if your employees use "company" cars to ensure that you can easily retrieve the information at the year end.

**5.** Make sure that forms P11D are completed and submitted on time – by 6 June.

**6.** Consider the Fixed Profit Car Scheme for employees using their own cars.

**7.** Give employees guidance notes if they do receive any taxable benefits, so that they understand the implications for the tax they pay.

**8.** Consider non-taxable benefits when discussing remuneration packages.

# STAFF EXPENSES CLAIM FORM

Name:_____ Month:_____

| Date | Voucher | Description/Reason | Amount £ | Travel £ | Books £ | Stationery £ | Canteen £ | Other £ | Notes |
|------|---------|--------------------|----------|----------|---------|--------------|-----------|---------|-------|
|  |  |  |  |  |  |  |  |  |  |
|  |  |  |  |  |  |  |  |  |  |
|  |  | TOTAL |  |  |  |  |  |  |  |

Claimed by_____ (signed)_____ (date) Approved by_____ (signed)_____ (date)

| MILEAGE CLAIM – Attach to Expenses Claim | | | |
|---|---|---|---|
| Date | Reason for Journey & Destination | Miles | £ |
| | | | |

Inland
**Revenue**

Employer's name _____  PAYE reference _____

Employee's/Director's name _____  NI number [ | | | | | | ]

## Notification of a car provided for the private use of an employee or a director

### Part 1

You are required to make a return on this form for an employee earning at the rate of £8,500 a year or more or a director for whom a car is made available for private use. The completed form is required within 28 days of the end of the quarter to 5 July, 5 October, 5 January or 5 April in which any of the following takes place.

*Tick whichever applies*

1.  The employee/director is first provided with a car which is available for private use ☐

2.  A car provided to the employee/director is replaced by another car which is available for private use ☐

3.  The employee/director is provided with a second or further car which is available for private use ☐

4.  The employee starts to earn at the rate of £8,500 a year or more or becomes a director ☐

5.  A car provided to the employee/director is withdrawn without replacement ☐

*Now please complete Part 2 overleaf*

**P46(Car)(1994)**

# Chapter 5

# NATIONAL INSURANCE

National insurance contributions are really another form of income tax, although they are different in as much as they are payable by both employee and employer. Contributions entitle individuals to pensions, sickness, maternity, unemployment and other benefits. It is therefore important that contributions are accurately recorded and submitted on the End of Year Returns to the central records of the Contributions Agency.

National insurance is collected by the Inland Revenue for the Contributions Agency of the Department of Social Security. Administration of national insurance contributions is undertaken as part of the PAYE system, but queries are dealt with by the Contributions Agency. This is part of the Department of Social Security and they produce guidance and run a helpline for employers.

The contributions paid under the PAYE system are known as Class 1 contributions. The amounts payable are described in "Tables 1" produced each year and sent automatically to every employer. Within this document, there are three categories of Class 1 contributions:

◆ Table A – standard rate

◆ Table B – reduced rate

◆ Table C – employer only

The figures given in the following paragraph refer to the "not contracted-out contributions" which should be used in most cases. Parallel tables are issued to those making contracted-out contributions applicable for those in approved pension schemes.

## Table A

Most employees contribute under Table A – standard rate. It applies to employees who are over age 16 and under pension age, 65 for men, 60 for women. It will apply to employees who have their own personal pension plan. For 1995/96, those earning above the lower earnings limit pay national insurance at 2% on the first £58 per week and then 10% on the next tranche of earnings up to an upper earnings limit of £440 a week. Employers contribute at a rate of 10.2% of gross pay with no upper earnings limit.

## Table B

The Table B rate of employee contributions at only 3.85% applies only to married women who elected for this rate many years ago. To use this table, you must receive a certificate of election (form CF383) or a certificate of reduced liability (form CF380A). No new certificates may be issued now and the scheme is being phased out.

## Table C

Employees over pension age do not have to contribute, although the employer still contributes at the standard rate. Use Table C for men aged 65 or over and women aged 60 or over. Employees of pension age should produce a certificate of age exception to allow you to use Table C. They may obtain a certificate by application to the Posting Check Group at the Contributions Agency, showing an original birth certificate as proof of their age.

You also use this table for employees who already contribute the maximum employee contributions in another employment. You need a form RD950 for such employees. The procedure for obtaining such a form is outlined below.

## Lower Earnings Limit

No national insurance is payable by employee or employer for employees earning at the rate of less than £58 per week (£251 per month) in 1995/96. There is a sliding scale for employer contributions on various levels of pay between £58 per week and £205 per week. Details of the contribution rates are given in the Tables 1.

## Upper Earnings Limit

Employees do not have to pay further contributions if they earn over £440 per week (£1,906 per month). Those earning at rates above this pay the maximum (£170.52 per month on Table A) and you should enter the upper earnings limit in column 1a on the P11, described as "Earnings on which employee's contributions payable". The employer has to pay full contributions on the total actual earnings (at 10.2%), as there is no upper earnings limit for employer contributions.

## Multiple Employments

Since national insurance is calculated on the pay in the week or month (not on a cumulative basis as for income tax), employees with more than one job could find that they are paying too much national insurance. There is an annual maximum employees are required to pay (£2,037.32 for 1994/95). Employees should automatically receive a refund once the Contributions Agency has collated all the details from end of year returns. Employees can obtain the refund more quickly if they write to the Contributions Agency (Refunds Group, Department of Social Security, Longbenton, Newcastle upon Tyne, NE98 1YX) sending P60's or payslips as evidence of the contributions deducted from pay.

Employers cannot obtain a refund and employer's contributions are always payable in full.

To avoid the need for contributions to be deducted from such employees when it is known that it will have to be refunded, an application can be made for authorisation for contributions to be deferred. (Using form CF379 in leaflet

CA 01 available from the Contributions Agency) In order for the scheme to be approved, there needs to be one or a combination of several employments which will clearly reach the upper earnings limit. The other employment(s) may then be exempt from employee contributions and those employers will be issued with form RD950. The employer still has to make contributions as usual and will use Table C.

## Contracted-Out Contributions

All the rates quoted above are the "not contracted-out" rates of national insurance contributions, which apply to employees who are not in an approved pension scheme. The contracted-out rates are lower than the normal rates, because the employees have contracted out of the State Earnings Related Pension Scheme (SERPS) and instead are part of an occupational pension scheme or superannuation scheme. You will only be able to use these lower rates if you have a contracted-out scheme number. You may not use the lower rates where employees have simply taken out personal pension plans, even though they may have contracted out of SERPS. Personal pension plans are not qualifying occupational pension schemes and the full rates of national insurance must be paid.

## Working Abroad

In general, national insurance contributions are still payable for the first 52 weeks that an employee spends working abroad. For this to apply, the following conditions have to be met:

◆ the employee is ordinarily resident, i.e. they were living in the UK before the work abroad and intend to return to the UK within five years.

◆ the employee was resident in the UK immediately before starting the work abroad.

◆ the employer has a "place of business" in the UK, i.e. is registered as a charity or company in the UK or has a branch in the UK

To avoid the 52 week liability, one of the conditions has to be broken, since all three are requirements.

For example, if you recruit someone overseas and they do not return to the UK before commencing employment, then there is no liability to pay national insurance for the first 52 weeks.

There are special arrangements where the UK has a reciprocal agreement, so you will need to check whether this applies to the country. These do change from time to time and you can check current information as well as the appropriate action to take by contacting the Overseas Branch (Department of Social Security, Longbenton, Newcastle, NE98 1YX).

You need to notify the Overseas Branch if you do pay national insurance contributions for the first 52 weeks and then cease to be liable, although still employing the person. The Overseas Branch will then keep the person informed direct of their contributions status. If an employee is working outside the European Union, then he or she will not be entitled to Statutory Sick Pay or Statutory Maternity Pay.

## Voluntary Contributions

If employees are not making any national insurance contributions, then this will affect their entitlement to benefits. They may safeguard their position to a certain extent by making voluntary contributions (Class 3 contributions). Class 3 contributions will only improve their entitlement to the basic retirement pension and widows' benefits. It will not entitle them to SERPS or unemployment benefit.

If an individual is registered unemployed or in receipt of sickness benefit, maternity allowance, incapacity allowance or certain other benefits, then they will be credited with national insurance contributions at a basic level. There is no need for them to make voluntary contributions.

## Employees from Abroad

Employees who are only in the UK on a temporary basis may be exempt from paying national insurance contributions, as would the employer. This can only apply to the first 52 weeks after the employee's arrival in the UK, and if the employment continues after this 52 week period then national insurance contributions must be paid as normal. This exemption can apply to employees of overseas organisations and overseas students working in their holidays for work experience. It will not apply to employees coming from other countries in the European Union and other countries with whom the UK has a reciprocal arrangement. You will need to check which countries are included under these arrangements, as they do change from time to time.

If in doubt about whether the exemption will apply or not, then contact your local Social Security office for guidance and deduct national insurance in the meantime.

## Earnings

National insurance contributions are payable on earnings. The definition of earnings is such that it includes many benefits in kind, as well as salary, bonuses, commission. There is no system for declaring the benefit for national insurance in the way that the tax system operates through the forms P11D. It is up to the employer to include the correct amount in column 1a on the Deductions Working Sheet P11 – "Earnings on which employee's contributions payable". This may mean that the amount of gross pay for tax purposes is different to the earnings on which national insurance contributions must be calculated.

For example, an employee contributing to the superannuation scheme (approved pension scheme) will have these contributions deducted from gross pay before taxable pay is calculated. National insurance contributions are payable on the full amount of gross pay before any deduction for superannuation contributions.

Earnings will include the following:

◆ salary or wages

◆ sick pay

◆ maternity pay

◆ commission

◆ bonuses

◆ incentive payments

◆ backdated pay increases

◆ allowances paid to employees (e.g. clothing allowances, meal allowances, childcare allowances)

◆ holiday pay

◆ loans written off by the employer or paid off on the employee's behalf

◆ payments on the employee's behalf (e.g. payments to their pension scheme, permanent health scheme)

◆ vouchers which can be redeemed for cash

## Other benefits

No national insurance contributions are payable on "true" benefits in kind. So you may give a present to an employee, or a voucher which is only exchangeable for goods (such as a store gift voucher) without a liability to national insurance arising. Payments by the employer direct will avoid potential liabilities. Hence it is better for the employer to buy any special clothing required and provide it for the employee's use, rather than giving the employee a cash allowance. An organisation can contract with an insurance company for permanent health cover for its employees and pay the premiums without any consequent liability for national insurance. If the employee enters into a contract for permanent health cover and the employer agrees to pay the premium, then this would be liable to national insurance and would have to be included in earnings.

## Expenses

No national insurance contributions are payable where the employer is merely reimbursing expenses incurred by the employee on the employer's behalf.

## National Insurance on cars and fuel

Cars provided to employees have long been taxed as a benefit in kind, but now employers have to pay additional national insurance contributions on the benefit as well. These are known as Class 1A national insurance contributions and these are explained in some detail in the Manual for Employers – Cars and Fuel CA 33 (NI 280).

Employers have to pay the Class 1A contributions if they provide a car to an employee earning at a rate of £8,500 or more or to a company director receiving remuneration. The contributions are only payable if the car is available to the employee for private use. This will include driving from home to work, as that is a private journey, not a business journey. Private use also includes the use of the car by a spouse or any relative. The Class 1A contributions are payable if there is a taxable benefit. So following those rules, there is no liability to Class 1A if the car is not available to the employee for private use or if the car is a "pool" car.

In the tax year 1993/94, the benefit subject to additional national insurance contributions was based on the scale charges used for tax purposes (see appendix). The employer would then have to calculate 10.4% of the scale charge that applied to work out the Class 1A contributions payable.

From the tax year 1994/95 onwards, the benefit will again follow the tax system and so will be based on the list price of the car.

## Fuel Benefits

Class 1A also applies to fuel provided by an employer to an employee when the car is being used for private use. If the employee reimburses the employer for fuel supplied for private use, then no Class 1A is payable. Class 1A contributions on fuel will be payable on a scale rate based on the age, size and original market value of the car, irrespective of the actual amount of fuel provided or the private mileage undertaken.

## Paying Class 1A Contributions

These are only payable after the end of the tax year by 19 June following the end of the tax year as part of your normal remittance for the May payroll (payable by 19 July if you are a small employer and remit quarterly). Interest is chargeable on late payment. You show the Class 1A contributions on the payroll documentation of the following year. For example, show the amounts paid on 19 June 1995 on forms P11, P14 and P35 for 1995/96, even though the contributions payable are calculated on the basis of cars and fuel for 1994/95.

## Alternative Payment Method

This is an option open to all employers now, although prior to 5 April 1994 it was only available to employers paying Class 1A contributions on ten or more cars. The Class 1A contributions are remitted direct to the Contributions Agency and are not shown on the payroll documentation at all. Application has to be made to the Contributions Agency on form CA34 before 5 April of the appropriate tax year and contributions are still payable by 19 June.

Reductions in Class 1A Contributions Where the car was only available for part of the year, then the benefit should be pro-rated. If the car is off the road for more than 30 consecutive days, then the benefit can also be reduced, but you should be able to prove that it was unavailable for use. For example, correspondence with a garage or insurance company should prove that a car was off the road. A reduction is available if the business miles are 18,000 or more, but you may need to produce evidence of the miles, such as a mileage record.

## Action Points – National Insurance

**1.** Ensure that you are using the correct tables.

**2.** Only use Table B if the employee gives you a certificate entitling them to reduced rates.

**3.** Only use Table C if the employee produces a certificate of age exception or employees with more than one job who produce a certificate RD950.

**4.** Only use the contracted out tables if the organisation has an occupational pension scheme and a contracted out number. Reduced contributions do not apply to those in personal pension plans.

**5.** Ensure that you have all details of payments and benefits which need to be included in earnings for national insurance purposes.

**6.** Remember Class 1A contributions when preparing year end returns and include these on P14's and P35. These are employer only contributions on car and fuel benefit.

**7.** If your organisation has to pay Class 1A contributions, include these in budgets, as they are an additional cost to the employer.

**8.** Make sure that you pay Class 1A contributions to Inland Revenue by 19 July.

**9.** Consider paying contributions direct to Contributions Agency and avoid the need for inclusion on P14 and P35. This will benefit those employers whose computer systems cannot calculate Class 1A contributions.

# Chapter 6
# VOLUNTEERS

Payments to volunteers may come under the PAYE rules and be liable to tax or they may be taxable benefits. To avoid tax liabilities, charities should only reimburse expenses to volunteers. Any payment for work done, even if it is a small amount, is potentially taxable. It will depend on the circumstances of the individual as to whether tax is payable or not. Expenses may be paid without causing any problems.

## Volunteer Status

If someone provides services to a charity on a voluntary basis, then they may not be paid at all for those services. If they are paid any amount, then their status as volunteers is jeopardised. They become employees if they are paid, even if they work irregular hours, part-time or on a temporary basis. The amount involved will not make any difference to the question of status, as it is quite possible for an employee to be paid at a low rate.

If volunteer status is lost, then the normal PAYE procedures apply and you should be putting payments through the payroll. You would have to ask people for their P45, or ask them to complete a form P46. If they have no other income and you are paying them less than the lower earnings limit for National Insurance (£58 in 1995/96), then in fact no deductions for tax and national insurance need to be made. However, problems will arise if the person involved is receiving a pension, as this counts as "other employment".

## Volunteer Status and Benefits

Many volunteers may be in receipt of welfare benefits of one sort or another. Certain individuals will be entitled to therapeutic earnings and you may therefore pay them up to this level (£15 at 1994 rates). This means that they should not suffer a reduction in their benefits.

Those in receipt of unemployment benefit or supplementary benefits because they are unemployed need to be careful that they are still available for work. Voluntary activity should not jeopardise their status, but these volunteers need to take care and ensure that they can attend interviews. They cannot commit themselves to any long term projects as they have to show that they could start work in a day or two. Similarly, those who are disabled and in receipt of incapacity allowance need to be careful. Voluntary activity might be interpreted as a demonstration that they are in fact capable of work. The rules have been tightened up in this area.

Charities and volunteers may be wise to seek advice before they go too far. Citizens Advice Bureaux are well qualified to advise individuals and volunteers. Charities may wish to consult The Volunteer Centre for advice on how to structure their volunteer programme. This is a complex area and the above is only an indication of potential problems.

## Volunteer Expenses

There is no problem in reimbursing a volunteer for the actual cost to them of travelling to the organisation. Similarly, volunteers may be reimbursed for the cost of their lunch. The amount paid should be a reimbursement, however, and therefore you need to ask for proper details. It is not necessary to have every bus ticket, but you should know the distance travelled and the method of transport. This would enable an independent check on the level of expense being paid if necessary.

## Record Keeping

It is important that proper records are kept in this area. A form should be devised and used for volunteer expenses, with any available receipts attached. The volunteer's name should be shown, the volunteer should sign for the expenses claimed and the claim should be approved by an appropriate person in the organisation (e.g. the volunteer co-ordinator).

It will not be enough to simply write "volunteer expenses" and the amount on a petty cash voucher. If investigated, this would probably be treated as a cash payment to an employee and tax and national insurance would be due, costing the organisation nearly 70% as much again. To avoid this situation, records should clearly show who the volunteers are (names and addresses) and that the amounts they have received are the reimbursement of expenses only.

## Flat Rate Allowances

Generally, flat rate allowances are taxable. For tax purposes, these are treated the same as payment for work. However, it may be possible to obtain the agreement of the local inspector of taxes to a maximum rate for expenses payments to volunteers. Providing the amount is small and reasonable given the amount of travelling and costs incurred by most volunteers, then effectively you can operate a flat rate payment scheme. Ensure that you get approval to a scheme beforehand and that you adhere to the terms of the scheme afterwards. The terms may restrict the circumstances in which such payments may be tax free. The rules about payment for work will still apply and a flat rate allowance should not be a disguised payment for work.

This will be of considerable benefit to organisations using a great number of volunteers and will save a significant amount of administrative time. There will be a need for some paperwork, however, and the notes about record keeping still apply to such schemes.

## Home-based Volunteers

Some volunteers operate from home and may need to claim for telephone, postage, stationery etc. This is quite acceptable, as long as the basic principle is still maintained that they are only reimbursed for expenses incurred in the course of their volunteering. For example, they should keep a log of telephone calls and only claim for the calls made. The rental of the telephone line and any equipment would presumably be costs incurred by the volunteer anyway, and therefore cannot be claimed as part of their volunteering expenses. Claim forms should be submitted and approved by an appropriate person or the treasurer.

## Volunteer Drivers

Volunteer drivers are entitled to reimbursement for their expenses on a mileage basis. Care must be exercised, however, that the mileage rate used does not lead to a taxable benefit. If the rate used is deemed to be high enough that the volunteer driver can make a profit from the activity, then the whole amount becomes taxable. Non-taxable mileage rates are set out each tax year in a table. The rates for 1994/95 are set out below. The rates vary depending on the size of the car and the number of miles travelled each year. The main problems arise if a volunteer driver does more than 4,000 miles per year in the course of their volunteering. The mileage rate should decrease as they do more miles, because some of their costs are presumably fixed (such as insurance and road fund licence) and they start to make a profit once those costs are covered.

Organisations using volunteer drivers need to give out clear guidance on how mileage allowances will be paid. They also need to set up a system which monitors the mileage of volunteer drivers in any one tax year. A cumulative total of the miles driven needs to be kept if it is at all likely that the threshold of 4,000 miles will be breached.

If these arrangements are not in place, then volunteer drivers may find themselves liable to tax on the "profit" element of the mileage allowances paid to them. Because the rule has not always applied to volunteer drivers, there are transitional rules to soften the tax blow. Any profit element will only be taxed as to three-quarters in 1994/95, but it will be taxed fully in 1995/96 and subsequent years.

## Non-Taxable Mileage Rates

These are the rates at which you may reimburse drivers for miles on the charity's behalf in their own vehicle:

### The non-profit rates in 1994/95 are:

|                  | to 4,000 miles in year | over 4,000 miles in year |
|------------------|------------------------|--------------------------|
| Up to 1,000 cc   | 27p                    | 15p                      |
| 1,001-1,500 cc   | 33p                    | 19p                      |
| 1,501-2,000 cc   | 41p                    | 23p                      |
| Over 2,000 cc    | 56p                    | 31p                      |

## Trustees and Management Committee Members

All charities will have volunteers on their management committee, who are the trustees of the charity. It is a requirement of charitable status that the trustees should receive no benefit from the charity. This prohibits them from being employees of the charity or being paid for their services as trustees. This requirement is being relaxed a little. New Charity Commission guidelines state that new charities may incorporate the payment of "reasonable" sums to their trustees in their constitution and existing charities may apply for permission from the Charity Commission to do so. Permission may be granted in certain circumstances, which are set out in a booklet available from the Charity Commission on the remuneration of trustees (CC11).

If your charity does pay trustees, then this would have to be disclosed in the accounts. (Statement of Recommended Practice; Accounting by Charities) Expenses paid to trustees will also need to be disclosed in a note to the accounts.

## Trustee Expenses

Trustees are entitled to be reimbursed for expenses incurred in the course of their duties. Trustees are consequently the same as other volunteers and the charity should ensure that trustees claim expenses on proper forms as for all volunteers.

It is usual for trustees to claim the following:

◆ travel expenses for attending meetings

◆ subsistence, e.g. hotel bills if they have to stay overnight to attend meetings or fulfil their duties as trustees

◆ the cost of training courses attended in their capacity as trainee

◆ reimbursement of costs incurred on behalf of the charity e.g. postage

◆ reimbursement of childcare costs while attending meetings

Refreshments are usually provided at meetings and these may be provided at the charity's expense. If one of the trustees provides these, then they may claim back the cost.

Under charity law, trustees may claim loss of earnings whilst undertaking their duties. For example, if a trustee has to take a day off their normal work because they are interviewing candidates for a job at the charity, then they may claim for the net pay they have foregone. Under tax law, however, this would amount to payment for work and would be taxable.

## High Levels of Expenses

Care is still needed even if you only reimburse expenses, but these are at high levels. This might arise in national and international charities where the trustees have to travel long distances to meetings and perhaps stay overnight in hotels. If the total expenses reimbursed amount to £8,500 in a tax year, then the charity has to complete a form P11D. This is a return of expenses payments and benefits. The trustee then has to make a corresponding claim on his or her tax return for the expenses, showing that the trustee had to pay that amount out and consequently made no profit.

The charity could pay for the travel and hotel costs direct to avoid this problem. Note, however, that the total amount of expenses should still be disclosed in a note to the accounts.

## Action Points – Volunteers and Trustees

**1.** Ensure that volunteers are reimbursed for the expenses they incur while volunteering.

**2.** Obtain Inland Revenue approval if you wish to use a flat rate payment scheme for volunteers.

**3.** Use volunteer expenses claim forms.

**4.** Keep a separate log of trustee expenses for inclusion in the annual accounts.

**5.** Prepare guidance notes for volunteers to explain to them what they may and may not claim.

**6.** Keep a list of volunteers showing their names and addresses.

**7.** Seek advice from the Citizen's Advice Bureau or other advisory group if you regularly use volunteers who may be in receipt of benefits, so that you can advise your volunteers.

# VOLUNTEER EXPENSES CLAIM FORM

Name: _____    Month: _____

| Date | Description/Reason | Amount £ | Travel £ | Lunch £ | Childcare £ | Telephone £ | Postage £ | Other £ | Notes |
|------|-------------------|----------|----------|---------|-------------|-------------|-----------|---------|-------|
|      |                   |          |          |         |             |             |           |         |       |
| TOTAL |                  |          |          |         |             |             |           |         |       |

Claimed by _____ (signed) _____ (date)   Approved by _____ (signed) _____ (date)

Chapter 7

# SICK PAY AND MATERNITY PAY

## SICK PAY

Employers are obliged to pay Statutory Sick Pay (SSP) to most employees once they have been ill for more than four consecutive days. The levels of SSP are low compared to most salaries and, in general, most employers pay their own occupational sick pay which is in excess of SSP. As long as the employer is meeting their obligation to pay the minimum, then SSP will not present an additional financial burden.

When first introduced, SSP was recoverable in full from national insurance contributions as well as an amount in compensation for the employer's contributions being paid on SSP. The value of SSP recovery has been gradually eroded as the rates of SSP have remained largely static, the compensation has been abolished, the rate of recovery has been reduced to 80% of SSP paid (applies to 93/94 tax year) and now no recovery of SSP is available in 1994/95, except for small employers.

## Small Employers' Relief

Small employers (in 1994/95) are those whose total national insurance contributions in the tax year 1993/94 amounted to £20,000 or less. This includes both employer's and employees' contributions before any SSP or SMP has been deducted. (Check the End of Year Return P35 for the correct figure.) If your organisation qualifies as a small employer, then you can recover 100% SSP once you have already paid four weeks of SSP to an employee. You cannot recover any of the first four weeks of SSP paid to an employee and so the recovery only applies to long term sickness. SSP is recovered by deducting the amount of SSP paid from the national insurance contributions due for the month. (Leaflet CA32 gives a few more details)

## Percentage Threshold Scheme

From 6 April 1995, the percentage threshold scheme will replace the small employers' relief. Under this scheme, any employer may recover some SSP when the amount of SSP due for the month exceeds 13% of the gross national insurance (excluding Class 1A) due for the month. The amount recoverable will be the excess SSP and it will be recovered by deduction from national insurance remittances.

## SSP Records

Even if SSP is no longer recoverable for your organisation, you will still need to keep adequate records to prove that you are complying with the rules. You still need to keep records of periods of sickness of four or more consecutive days, the days for which SSP was payable, the amount of SSP paid or cases where SSP was not paid and the reasons why. This is not only a legal requirement, but situations could arise where an employee is no longer entitled to sick pay under the contract of employment and you will only be paying SSP, if eligible, or the employee will have to claim sickness benefit direct from the Benefits Agency.

For those operating manual systems, it will be simplest to keep records of all absences on a record sheet available from the local Social Security office, form SSP2. These can be readily kept with the Deductions Working Sheet (P11) for each employee.

You also need to obtain self-certificates of sickness from employees for absences of between four and seven days. A doctor's certificate is required if the absence is more than seven days.

## SSP Terminology

**PIW**  Period of incapacity for work – a period of sickness lasting four or more days in a row. These are not necessarily normal working days, but can include weekends or holidays.

**Qualifying days**  the days on which an employee is normally expected to work and for which SSP may be paid. For many full-time staff the qualifying days will be Monday to Friday inclusive. For staff working on different days each week because they work shifts or on a rota, it may be more appropriate for the qualifying days to be Sunday to Saturday. It makes no difference if staff only work part days, you still look at the days they normally work to establish the qualifying days. It is useful to state the qualifying days in the contract of employment, so that there is no confusion.

**Waiting days**  the first three days of a period of incapacity for work are "waiting days" and no SSP is payable.

**Linking**  periods of sickness will be linked for SSP purposes if they are separated by eight weeks or less. Note that they have to be PIW's, that is periods of sickness each lasting four or more days and that they do not have to be medically linked. It does not matter if the cause for the absence is a different ailment. The effect is that the absences are treated as one PIW for SSP purposes and further waiting days are not necessary. You have to check for linking PIW's when new employees are absent due to sickness for four days or more within the first eight weeks of their employment with you. Ask the employee for their leaver's statement (Form SSP1(L) which they should have received from their previous employer if they were paid at least four days SSP in the last eight weeks of their employment.

## How It Works

An employee rang the office to tell you she would be absent due to sickness on Monday and is likely to be absent for a few days. You send her a self-certificate, which she completes and returns. This shows that she became ill on the Sunday. She is still not fit for work after seven days of illness and so goes to her doctor at the first opportunity and obtains a certificate for a further one week's sick leave. Qualifying days are Monday to Friday in her job.

You mark the sick days on the record sheet, identifying the non- qualifying days as you do so and marking them "N":

Sunday      N
Monday
Tuesday
Wednesday
Thursday
Friday
Saturday    N
Sunday      N
Monday
Tuesday
Wednesday
Thursday
Friday
Saturday    N

Next you need to check that there is no linked PIW in the preceding eight weeks. (There is no previous sickness) In this case, you need to allow three waiting days (marked "W") and then mark the record for SSP days on subsequent qualifying days using "P".

Sunday      N
Monday          W
Tuesday         W
Wednesday       W
Thursday            P
Friday              P
Saturday    N
Sunday      N
Monday              P
Tuesday             P
Wednesday           P
Thursday            P
Friday              P
Saturday    N

Seven days of SSP should be paid. Because the terms and conditions of employment provide for full pay for sickness for a maximum of three months, then you will in fact be paying this employee her full gross pay. This should be entered as usual on the P11, but you must also enter the amount of SSP entitlement. The rate of SSP applicable will be either the lower rate or higher rate, depending on the employee's weekly pay. Calculate the daily rate using the SSP tables sent at the beginning of each tax year. SSP does not need to be paid in addition to the normal gross pay, but is deemed to be included in the gross pay and is taxed and subject to national insurance. You do not qualify as a small employer and therefore no SSP can be recovered. It must still be recorded on the P11 and the P14 at the end of the year.

## No SSP Payable

There are situations where the SSP rules do not provide for payment of SSP. Employers may still choose to pay sick pay under their own terms, and may be obliged to do so if the contract of employment requires it.

No SSP is payable if:

- ◆ the employee earns less than the lower earnings limit
- ◆ the employee is on a fixed term contract for three months or less
- ◆ the employee is outside the European Union and countries in the European Economic Area
- ◆ the employee is entitled to Statutory Maternity Pay
- ◆ the employee is on strike
- ◆ the employee is over 65 years of age
- ◆ the employee is in prison
- ◆ the employee has already been sick for 28 weeks
- ◆ the employee had a recent claim to sickness benefit, invalidity benefit, severe disablement allowance or maternity allowance
- ◆ the employee had not actually started work

If no SSP can be paid, then a change-over form (SSP1) should be issued. This may entitle the employee to benefits direct from the social security office (Benefits Agency).

## General Guidance on Sick Pay

Employers need to ensure that they have appropriate procedures to record sickness. This is not simply for SSP purposes, but as a matter of good internal control. More employers are realising that sickness costs an organisation a great deal, even when the absences are just the odd day. Under the SSP rules, self certificates are required for illnesses lasting four days or more, until the sickness has lasted seven days, after which a doctor's certificate is required. For entitlement to full pay under your own sick pay scheme, you can request that self certificates are submitted for all absences due to sickness, however short. You may also require a doctor's certificate earlier or for repeated absences. (Some doctors may initially refuse to give a certificate if the illness is less than seven days.) You must make it clear that any in-house rules are for entitlement to additional sick pay, as employees are entitled to SSP providing those rules are adhered to.

Employers also need to be aware of how the rules apply to part-time employees, where contracts of employment are not always so generous. You also need to examine all contracts of employment to check that the terms do fit in with the SSP rules. You may not exclude any category of employees from SSP by a clause in the contract of employment, but see the list above for situations where SSP does not apply.

Employers need to have clear guidelines on the policy and procedure for the many potentially difficult situations which may arise in relation to sick leave. It can be difficult for trustees to be suddenly faced with a grievance or a decision, so it is far better to set out such matters in guidance notes or a staff manual. Examples of situations which need policy are given below:

◆ doctor's appointment for non-urgent matter

◆ dental check-up

◆ attendance at antenatal clinic

◆ optician's appointments

◆ appointments for acupuncture, homeopathic treatment or other complimentary medicine

◆ repeated absences of one day or two days

◆ long-term illness or disability

◆ absence because of a sick relative being claimed as sick leave

◆ sickness while on annual leave

Note that SSP can only be paid if the employee is incapable of work. An employer's policy may cover payment where SSP would not be due, such as regular check-ups.

## Permanent Health Insurance

A benefit which many employers provide is payment of premiums for permanent health insurance. This is rather a misnomer, as it is insurance which pays out in the event of long-term sickness. You may choose from a policy which starts to pay out after four weeks of illness, or thirteen weeks of illness or other periods. Premiums will be higher if the pay out starts earlier. The pay out is usually tied to gross salary, being a proportion of the salary.

The payout can either go direct to the employee or it can go to the employer. If the employer is going to top up the payout, then it is easier if the payout goes to the employer. The whole amount paid to the employee is then taxable in the normal way. In this situation, the premiums are not a taxable benefit, since it is the employer who is obtaining insurance cover for the cost of long-term sickness.

On the other hand, if the employee receives the payout from the policy direct, then this will not be taxable for the first year. The premiums will have been paid on the employee's behalf and are therefore a taxable benefit.

Clearly, employers need to consider the terms in the contract of employment. If there is an obligation to pay full pay for a substantial period of sickness (e.g. six months) then it may well be worth obtaining insurance cover. If there is no obligation to pay employees beyond SSP during long illnesses, then permanent health insurance where the employee receives the benefit will be a useful "perk" to the employee.

Policies vary enormously and proper advice needs to be sought from a financial adviser. The conditions and terms of the policy need to be considered carefully to check that the policy will, in fact, pay out in the situations most likely to occur.

## MATERNITY PAY

In a similar way to sick pay, there is a statutory scheme which employers are obliged to operate, but they may have more generous terms if they so wish. Statutory Maternity Pay (SMP) has been in operation for several years, but changes are being introduced during the tax year 1994/95 affecting women expecting babies on or after 16 October 1994.

SMP is payable at two rates: a higher rate and a lower rate. The higher rate is 90% of average earnings for six weeks, followed by the lower rate for a further 12 weeks. The lower rate is a set rate fixed for each tax year in the November budget. SMP is payable if a woman qualifies whether or not she intends to return to work for you. SMP is taxable and subject to national insurance contributions.

To qualify for SMP, a woman has to fulfil a set of conditions. Note that all the conditions must be satisfied:

◆ she must have been continuously employed by you for 26 weeks continuing into the fifteenth week before the baby is due

◆ she must be earning above the lower earning limit for National Insurance contributions

◆ still be pregnant at the eleventh week before the baby is due or have had the baby

◆ give you a form (MATB1) signed by a doctor or midwife as evidence of the date the baby is due at least 21 days before the maternity leave is due to commence

◆ she must have stopped working before SMP can be paid

If a woman does not qualify for SMP because she fails to meet one of the conditions above, then you should give her a form SMP 1. She may then be able to claim Maternity Allowance.

## SMP Terminology

| | |
|---|---|
| **Expected Week of Confinement** | the week in which the baby is due. Weeks always begin on a Sunday. |
| **Qualifying Week** | this is the fifteenth week before the week in which the baby is due. |
| **Maternity Pay Period** | the period during which SMP is paid or should be paid |
| **Average Weekly Earnings** | these have to be calculated by the formula in the SMP guide. Average weekly earnings must be above the lower earnings limit for the woman to qualify for SMP. |

## Calculation of Average Weekly Earnings

Since SMP is based on average weekly earnings, it is important that the calculation is undertaken correctly. You need to look for paydays in the eight weeks up to and including the last payday before the end of the qualifying week. You then average the gross pay before deductions. Gross pay may include bonuses, allowances, back pay and should be before any deductions such as superannuation.

For a monthly paid employee, you would add the gross pay for the two paydays before the qualifying week, then multiply by six (to obtain annual equivalent) and divide by 52 (to obtain weekly equivalent). This provides you with the average weekly earnings figure. This must be greater than the lower earnings limit for SMP to be paid at all. SMP will be due at 90% of this amount for the first six weeks of the maternity leave.

Take care that you use the gross pay from the correct months (or weeks). A common mistake is to base SMP on the rate of pay at the time the Maternity Pay Period commences. It may also be incorrect to just take the annual pay, since there may be adjustments to the gross pay in the particular months which should be considered.

The rate of SMP can therefore be affected by the amount paid to an employee when she is four to six months pregnant. For example, a part-time employee could increase her hours for those two months.

Note that SMP should be calculated at the appropriate weekly rates, even if you pay someone monthly. You will probably find it easier to use form SMP2 for keeping a record of the weekly SMP due. You may then enter the SMP for the month in the normal way and process salaries as normal. Some months, four weeks of SMP will be due and some months five weeks of SMP will be due.

## Differences between the Old Rules and the New Rules

Under the old rules, a woman had to be employed for two years full-time (working at least 16 hours a week) or five years part- time (working at least 8 hours a week) into the qualifying week to be eligible for the higher rate of SMP. This condition has been abolished and far more women will now qualify for the higher rate, only needing to work for 26 weeks into the qualifying week.

Under the old rules, a woman had to commence her Maternity Pay Period six weeks before the baby was due in order to receive the full 18 weeks of SMP. This rule has been abolished and the woman may continue to work for as long as she likes.

Under the new rules only "small employers" will be able to claim 100% of SMP and the employer's compensation at a rate of 4% of SMP paid. A small employer in 1995/96 will have paid no more than £20,000 in total National Insurance contributions in 1994/95 (employees and employers contributions). Other employers may only recover 92% of the SMP paid and no compensation is due at all.

---

### Action Points – Sick Pay and Maternity Pay

**1.** Check whether your organisation qualifies as a small employer for current tax year.

**2.** Ensure that staff know that they must use self-certificates for absences due to sickness. Consider when you want them to use these. SSP rules mean that you must have them for absences of between four and seven days, but you may request them for all absences.

**3.** Agree policy on matters such as dental appointments.

**4.** Agree policy on sickness while on annual leave.

**5.** Ensure that you have a system for recording absences, possibly using forms SSP2.

**6.** Check that contracts of employment are clear about the amount of paid sick leave.

**7.** Set up a system for monitoring the amount of paid sick leave.

**8.** Devise a procedure for dealing with situations where the employee takes excessive sick leave.

---

## SELF CERTIFICATE OF ILLNESS

Name _____

Department _____

Last day of work _____ day _____ (date) _____ (month)

First day back at work _____ day _____ (date) _____ (month)

Total number of days off _____

Reason for absence:




Employee_____ (signed) _____ (date)


**For Office Use**

Number of qualifying days

Does this link to a previous Period of Incapacity for Work? _____ Yes / No

Sickness record updated _____ (initial) _____ (date)

# STATUTORY SICK PAY
## Record sheet

**SSP**

Employee's name

Tax year

**2** Maximum SSP liability

| Days | Money |
|------|-------|
| | £ |

**Information brought forward**

A Date excluded from SSP with you
B Last day of PIW
C First day of sickness in PIW

| | Money |
|---|-------|
| | £ |
| | £ |
| | £ |

**D** Rate of SSP paid in PIW with you — Standard / Middle / Lower — 1 / 2 / 3

**E** Waiting days in PIW with you

**1** Tick qualifying days

| | Sun | Mon | Tue | Wed | Thu | Fri | Sat | Date |
|---|---|---|---|---|---|---|---|---|
| | ☐ | ☐ | ☐ | ☐ | ☐ | ☐ | ☐ | |
| | ☐ | ☐ | ☐ | ☐ | ☐ | ☐ | ☐ | |
| | ☐ | ☐ | ☐ | ☐ | ☐ | ☐ | ☐ | |

**3** Issue SSP·1(T) (transfer form) after

| Days | | Money |
|------|---|-------|
| | | £ |

**4** Record of sickness and SSP

| Week | Week ending Saturday | Sun | Mon | Tue | Wed | Thu | Fri | Sat | **5** SSP Due in week/month | **6** Running total of SSP | **7** Remarks |
|---|---|---|---|---|---|---|---|---|---|---|---|
| 27 | | | | | | | | | | | |
| 28 | | | | | | | | | | | |
| 29 | | | | | | | | | | | |
| 30 | | | | | | | | | | | |
| 31 | | | | | | | | | | | |
| 32 | | | | | | | | | | | |
| 33 | | | | | | | | | | | |
| 34 | | | | | | | | | | | |
| 35 | | | | | | | | | | | |
| 36 | | | | | | | | | | | |
| 37 | | | | | | | | | | | |
| 38 | | | | | | | | | | | |
| 39 | | | | | | | | | | | |
| 40 | | | | | | | | | | | |
| 41 | | | | | | | | | | | |
| 42 | | | | | | | | | | | |
| 43 | | | | | | | | | | | |
| 44 | | | | | | | | | | | |
| 45 | | | | | | | | | | | |
| 46 | | | | | | | | | | | |
| 47 | | | | | | | | | | | |
| 48 | | | | | | | | | | | |
| 49 | | | | | | | | | | | |
| 50 | | | | | | | | | | | |
| 51 | | | | | | | | | | | |
| 52 | | | | | | | | | | | |
| * | | | | | | | | | | | |

\* Use this line if sickness at end of tax year includes part of a 53rd week.

## How to use this record sheet — continued

**Box 4** Use these code letters to note the days of sickness —

- **W** Waiting days
- **N** Non-qualifying days
- **X** Excluded. Give the reasons in Box 7
- Sickness in doubt, or late notification. Give the reasons in Box 7
- **T** Transferred
- **P** SSP is due. Only use **P** where the qualifying days vary. **If they do not vary,** write in the numbers.

Always note 4 days or more of sickness, whether or not SSP is due.

**If the qualifying days are the same each week**
- Use the **Days** parts of Boxes 2 and 3
- Note the days of SSP due in numbers. Write 1, 2, 3, 4, 5 etc in Box 4
- If the qualifying days change, write in the new details in Boxes 1, 2 and 3

**If the qualifying days are not the same each week**
- Use the **Money** parts of Boxes 2 and 3
- Write '**P**' in Box 4 for each day SSP is due
- Keep a running total of SSP in Box 6

At the beginning of a new tax year, start a new record sheet. Write in the new details for Boxes 2 and 3.

If a new employee gives you a leaver's statement that can be used, add its information to Boxes 2 and 3.

If SSP is due after a gap of more than 8 weeks, work out new details for Boxes 2 and 3.

105
182
59
79 to 90,
106 to 110
156 to 160

152

143

112

143

Printed in the UK for HMSO 8936673 3/000M 1 86 46086

Form SSP2

# Part B  Record of Maternity Pay Period

**Employee's name**

**National Insurance number**

**Tax year(s)**  /    /

### The Maternity Pay Period
The Maternity Pay Period (MPP) is the time when you could pay SMP.
It cannot be longer than 18 weeks although it may be shorter than 18 weeks.
▲ The quick guide to SMP (Yellow Book or NI268) will tell you more about this.

You must keep a record of this period even if your employee cannot get SMP for any week or does not come back to work when her baby is born. But if you exclude her completely from SMP at the beginning of the MPP you only need to fill in the first week of the record.

| Sunday of MPP week | Tax week No | Worked / Paid / Excluded | Amount of SMP paid | Running total of SMP | Notes |
|---|---|---|---|---|---|
| MPP weeks always begin on a Sunday. Note the date of each week until the MPP ends. | Show number of tax week MPP week is in. | Tick one box for each week. W = worked, P = paid SMP, E = excluded from SMP. Put reasons in Notes column. | Show how much SMP paid in each week. | This will help you to see quickly how much SMP you can get back | Note here any exclusion reasons. |
| 1 / / | | W P E | £ . | £ . | |
| 2 / / | | W P E | £ . | £ . | |
| 3 / / | | W P E | £ . | £ . | |
| 4 / / | | W P E | £ . | £ . | |
| 5 / / | | W P E | £ . | £ . | |
| 6 / / | | W P E | £ . | £ . | |
| 7 / / | | W P E | £ . | £ . | |
| 8 / / | | W P E | £ . | £ . | |
| 9 / / | | W P E | £ . | £ . | |
| 10 / / | | W P E | £ . | £ . | |
| 11 / / | | W P E | £ . | £ . | |
| 12 / / | | W P E | £ . | £ . | |
| 13 / / | | W P E | £ . | £ . | |
| 14 / / | | W P E | £ . | £ . | |
| 15 / / | | W P E | £ . | £ . | |
| 16 / / | | W P E | £ . | £ . | |
| 17 / / | | W P E | £ . | £ . | |
| 18 / / | | W P E | £ . | £ . | |

Chapter 8

# ACCOUNTING AND PAYROLL ADMINISTRATION

## INTERNAL CONTROLS

Salaries are frequently the largest expense for charities and therefore adequate controls need to be in place to ensure that the correct amounts are paid to employees and the PAYE system operated correctly.

## Authorisation

Charities need to have clear lines of authority for all personnel changes. In small charities, the trustees or management committee should approve new appointments and changes in pay rates. This approval should be documented in the minutes of the meeting and passed on to the person operating the payroll. In any size charity it is wise to document changes properly and to separate decision-making from implementation. For example, the person operating the payroll should only change the rates of pay when they receive a proper authorisation. The example form for change of employee details could be used.

## Security of payment

Very few employers these days pay employees cash in a wages packet. Many still draw individual cheques, although most larger employers use bank transfers. Cheques are more time-consuming and the risk of cheques being stolen or misused is high. More and more payments are being made direct from one bank account to another. The payment of monthly salaries is ideally suited to this system and your bank should be able to advise you on how to establish the system. The details of each employee's bank are kept on a master file and each month the payroll administrator completes the amount of net pay to be transferred. The total amount to be transferred needs to be authorised and signed by cheque signatories, just as if a cheque were being drawn for that amount.

## Segregation of Duties

In smaller charities there are often problems because the payroll administrator also undertakes many other tasks, such as bookkeeping, such that segregation of duties is a problem. At a minimum, the cheque signatories should not include the payroll administrator/bookkeeper. The treasurer or other cheque signatory should ask to see the salaries summary or wages book as documentary evidence to support the payments they are authorising. They should check that the payments look reasonable and that unusual payments are explained. They may sign the salaries book to indicate that they have reviewed it.

Good internal control systems will also operate a check on the end of year summaries before they are submitted to the Inland Revenue. Someone else should check the summaries for their accuracy and completeness, by totalling them and checking them back to the records. For example, check that all employees who have left during the year have been included as well as current employees.

## Accounting Controls

Accounting systems should incorporate control accounts for the main payroll accounts. For very small charities, this might only be done at the end of the year when the accounts are prepared. Where possible, however, monthly control accounts and reconciliations improve the internal controls. The main control accounts to set up are for the amounts due to the Inland Revenue and net pay. Additional control accounts may be set up following the same principles if you make other deductions from employees such as pension contributions or union dues. Once the payroll has been prepared, the total net pay due to the employees is entered on the credit side of the Net Pay Control Account. The total due to the Inland Revenue is entered on the credit side of the Inland Revenue Control Account. The sum of these two amounts is entered on the debit side of the Total Staff Costs Account (or a departmental analysis of total staff costs if that is how your system accounts for salary costs). This means that the cost entered into your accounting system includes both the gross pay and the employer's national insurance, as it should do.

The balance on the Net Pay Control Account should be cleared as payments to employees are entered onto the account. The payment to the Inland Revenue (due by 19th of the month following the payday) will clear the Inland Revenue Control Account. If there is a balance left on either of these accounts, then an error has been made and should be investigated.

## Preventing Fraud

The payroll is a potential target for fraud and charities are just as vulnerable in this respect as other employers. Some typical examples of fraud are:

◆ fictitious employee on payroll

◆ falsified overtime claims, timesheets, etc.

◆ theft of pay cheques

Clearly the priority will be to prevent fraud rather than to simply detect fraud after it has been committed. Some the procedures mentioned above are designed to prevent fraud as well as errors. Specifically some procedures will assist in preventing fraud:

The proper authorisation of new employee details and the proper administration of employees leaving will help to ensure that fictitious employees are not being paid on the payroll. This may be particularly important where there are several different locations for the organisation. The payroll administrator cannot be expected to know everyone, but someone should be in charge of the personnel function (even if your organisation is not large enough to employ a personnel officer). That person should be responsible for recording and passing to the payroll administrator details of changes. Good cross referencing between the personnel and payroll functions can reduce the risk of fraud in this area. Special attention should be paid to the procedures for temporary staff.

Senior staff should be responsible for authorising timesheets or overtime claims. They should be properly briefed so that they understand what the task involves and give it their proper attention. There should be back-up procedures to deal with the situation when the person who would normally authorise timesheets or overtime claims is absent. Payroll should have specimen signatures of those who may authorise timesheets and procedures should allow for these to be checked.

The use of cash or cheques should be avoided where possible. However, it will be necessary in certain cases. It is preferable if the pay can be collected or delivered in person. The payee should sign a form to indicate that they have received the pay. Sending cheques through the post is not very secure, as many cheques do get stolen. There may well be problems if the payee claims that they have not received their pay, but there is no proof that it was sent, delivered or stolen by a third party.

## Loans

Loans to employees should be limited in number and value. A charity should only be using its income for charitable purposes. If the trustees do, however, agree a policy which allows loans to staff in certain circumstances, then there should be a proper procedure for dealing with them.

The reason for the loan needs to be established. The trustees may decide that loans may be made to certain employees for the purchase of a vehicle, as they need one for the proper performance of their duties. Before the loan is advanced and the vehicle bought, the employee should sign a loan agreement. This should allow for the repayment of the loan by instalments and by deduction from the employee's net pay. A senior employee or a trustee should also specifically authorise the loan and sign the agreement.

The trustees will also need to consider the amount they are prepared to advance. Loans to staff should not cause the charity financial problems and clearly if resources are limited the trustees may need to suspend all further loans. The amount should not be more than an employee can repay over a reasonable period of time. Trustees need to consider how the loan would be repaid if the employee left.

A ledger account will need to be established to show the loan as a creditor, with transfers form the net pay control as the loan is paid off in instalments.

Usually, the auditors will require a signed certificate from staff at the financial year end confirming the balance outstanding.

## COMPUTERISED SYSTEMS

The payroll function can be readily computerised, as the same processes are required each month and the system is broadly the same for all employers. Consequently, there are numerous packages available for virtually any system. Most of these will perform quite adequately, but it is worth spending a little time making enquiries rather than just buying the cheapest.

1. Does the package come from a recognised supplier of software with an established track record?
2. Can we obtain references from any other users of the package?
3. If we need it, can the package process weekly as well as monthly payments?
4. Does the package produce all the forms, including year end documentation, in a form which is acceptable to the Inland Revenue?
5. Do they automatically send new tax tables etc. for installation onto the system, or do we have to pay an extra fee for this service?
6. Do they provide support in the event of problems and do we have to pay for this?
7. Can the package cope with extra numbers of staff if we expand a great deal?
8. Can the system transfer basic data on employees from one tax year to the next, or does this have to be entered again at the beginning of a new tax year?
9. How does the system cope with temporary staff?
10. Can the system produce a net pay listing which will show the bank details for direct credit (BACS listing) for use by the bank?
11. If necessary, can the system be run for more than one employer? (In the event that your organisation sets up a separate company or wants to run the payroll for other organisations as a service.)
12. Can the system provide you with the departmental analysis and management information you require?
13. Can the system produce information for forms P11D (if you require it)?

You will also need to check that the system can cope with your requirements on matters such as pensions. You would expect any system to have facilities for SSP, SMP and all aspects of the PAYE system.

### Should We Computerise?

It is difficult to state when an organisation should consider computerisation. The benefits are obvious when an organisation has a large number of staff. Smaller organisations may decide to computerise when they have, say, 20 staff so that the system is already running smoothly when they expand to 50 staff. An organisation with a complex payroll (for example, overtime payments, different hourly rates, lots of temporary staff) may benefit because the computer will perform the calculations accurately and reliably once the basic data is input to the system. If you only run a simple payroll where the same staff are paid the same amount each month, then you may find that you can prepare the payroll manually very quickly. It may also be a tedious, repetitive task to you that you would prefer to run on the computer! To a large extent, the decision is dependent on personal preference. For smaller organisations, a computer package will not cost a great deal and will not require a dedicated computer.

## Security and Controls in a Computerised System

You should consider the impact on the controls needed when you operate a computer based payroll system.

Data needs to be safeguarded from corruption, whether accidental or deliberate. Most payroll systems work with a master file, which holds information about the employees, pay rates, tax rates and so on. The system refers to this information when you run the payroll and it is therefore important that this data is accurate. You should restrict access to these files to authorised personnel only and ensure that regular back up copies are maintained. At least one back up copy should be held off site in the event of fire.

The information held for payroll purposes is also confidential. It is therefore usual for access to read as well as write information is restricted.

To be effective, passwords need to be changed from time to time, so that access is, in fact, restricted.

There need to be proper controls over manual payments made outside the system. A proper timetable for the processing of timesheets, overtime payments, temporary and weekly paid staff needs to be established which will minimise the need for manual payments. There is a risk that payments will be made twice or inaccurate payments made.

## Data Protection Act

If you do operate a payroll on a computerised system, then you should check whether you need to be registered under the Data Protection Act. For very simple payroll systems, this may not be necessary, but frequently the type of personnel information which is retained as part of the system does make registration necessary.

## USING A PAYROLL SERVICE

A significant number of organisations use a bureau or payroll service. Such services are offered by banks, accountants and some community accountancy projects or councils for voluntary service. The basis for charges for the service will vary, but it is common for a set-up charge to be made per employee, then a lower recurring charge per employee for routine payroll functions. You need to weigh up the advantages and disadvantages to your organisation, but the following are all factors which should be considered when making your decision.

Advantages:

◆ expertise available in PAYE matters

◆ reliable service producing payslips and end of year information on time

◆ time and expense saved as organisation does not have to buy software or employ staff for payroll preparation

◆ independence of payroll function and good segregation of duties

◆ good security of systems

Disadvantages:

◆ information not readily available if off site

◆ someone in the organisation still has to prepare the basic data for the bureau and communicate this to them

◆ errors may be made if information is not passed on efficiently, for example, sick leave

◆ cost (probably £50 per employee per year at least, and more if you use the services of a bank or other commercial provider)

◆ the bureau may require basic data well in advance of payroll preparation. This may mean that you have more manual payments to make because of lack of flexibility.

You may decide to use a bureau for a few years and then bring the service in-house when you have had time to train staff or when the organisation reaches a size where the bureau is uneconomic.

If you do decide to use a payroll service, then the best option to try first is your local Council for Voluntary Service. You must check that they run an efficient and competent service at a reasonable price. Your own auditors may also provide such a service and their charges may be reasonable if they provide you with other services.

There have been a couple of incidents of the payroll service itself going into liquidation in recent years. It would be extremely unwise to actually pass over money to the payroll service, unless you are using a bank or similar large and reputable establishment. It is better that your own organisation makes payments to employees and the Inland Revenue based on the payslips and monthly summaries provided by the service.

## Compliance Visits and PAYE Audits

Regular compliance visits are made by officers from a special section of the Inland Revenue. They will visit routinely every two years as a rule, but this will depend on the workload in your area and the priority cases they have. They are more likely to visit you more frequently if you employ subcontractors in the building trade and a large number of casual staff.

Inland Revenue inspectors are entitled to examine all your books and records and will not simply look at the payroll documentation itself. They will want to see cash books and petty cash, as well as invoices. This is when they will discover that you are not operating the PAYE system properly for the cleaner or a temporary member of staff you thought was self-employed. You will receive a bill (assessment) for the unpaid tax and national insurance in this situation.

If they do discover widespread non-compliance, then you may face more severe penalties. For example, if it is found that you have been making a large number of casual payments improperly, then they will make an assessment of the tax and national insurance due for the current or preceding tax year. They may then also assume that the same practice has been continuing for the last six years and therefore multiply the bill by six. You may not be told that they will do this at the time of the visit, but you will be sent the calculations and the total assessment in a letter after their visit. It comes as a great shock to many employers that this is legal. It is up to the employer to produce evidence to refute the calculations. In practice, this will mean going through the accounting records for the last six years in great detail, compiling a list of all cash payments. If you can identify the payees and produce evidence of their status, such as a P46 to show that it was their only job, then you may well be able to show that the tax bill should be much lower. Similarly, the exercise will be worthwhile if casual staff were only used in very recent years and you know that the cash payments in earlier years were much lower.

The issue of penalties will usually be decided at a later date, after the amount of tax due is agreed. The Inland Revenue will waive penalties altogether if they receive your co-operation and they believe that the non-compliance arose as a genuine mistake, rather than deliberate evasion of tax. This is a matter for their discretion, however. Penalties are usually calculated as a percentage of the tax due.

## DSS Audits

You will receive separate visits to check that you are collecting national insurance correctly and operating the SSP and SMP rules properly. The inspectors will be checking that Class 1 national insurance contributions are calculated on the correct earnings figure (including any benefits, if applicable). They will need to see your certificate for contracted out status if you have one. They will also be checking that Class 1A contributions are being calculated and paid over correctly for all employees with cars or fuel benefit. You will need to produce sickness records and the appropriate certificates and records for employees in receipt of SMP.

### Action Points – Administration and Controls

**1.** Ensure that all changes in staffing are notified to the finance section.

**2.** Ensure that all changes in pay are authorised by the trustees (or senior charity official if a very large organisation).

**3.** Try to establish a system whereby someone else checks the payroll.

**4.** Make sure that the bookkeeper is not also authorising salary rate changes and payments, such as signing cheques.

**5.** Set up accounting controls such as Inland Revenue control account and net pay control account.

**6.** Pay staff through the banking system rather than by cash or cheque.

**7.** Ensure that the organisation has clear loans policies and procedures.

## SAMPLE LOAN AGREEMENT

(*Name of Charity*) agrees to lend £ _____ to (*Name of Employee*)

for the purpose of _____

Interest will be charged at (*rate*) %.

(*Name of Employee*) agrees to repay the loan by (*number of instalments*)

monthly instalments of £ _____ each.

(*Name of Employee*) agrees that the amount of the loan repayment may be
deducted from their NET salary each month.

Signed on behalf of the charity          Signed by the employee

_____          _____

Date _____             Date _____

# STAFF CHANGES NOTIFICATION FORM

**Employee Name:**

---

**Details of change:**

Date started employment _____

Date terminates employment _____

Date salary changes to  £ _____

Effective Date _____

Other:




Authorised by _____

_____ Date

Implemented _____ Initials/Date

**NEW EMPLOYEE DETAILS**

1. Name: _____

2. Address: _____

   _____

   _____

3. Date of Birth: _____

4. National Insurance Number: _____

5. Bank Account Name: _____

   Bank Sort Code: _____

   Bank Account Number: _____

## SAMPLE PERSONNEL RECORD

Name: _____

Address: _____

_____

_____

Telephone: _____

Date Employment Started: _____ Terminated _____

Date Contract of Employment Signed: _____

Annual Salary: _____

At Commencement: _____

Reviews:                       date: _____

## Appendix

# TAX AND NATIONAL INSURANCE RATES

### Tax rates in 1994/95

| | | |
|---|---|---|
| Lower rate income tax | 20% | applies to taxable income up to £3,000 |
| Basic rate income tax | 25% | applies to taxable income from £3,001 to £23,700 |
| Higher rate income tax | 40% | applies to taxable income over £23,701 |

### Allowances in 1994/95

| | | |
|---|---|---|
| Single personal allowance | £3,445 | |
| Additional (for married men or person with a dependent child) | £1,720 | relief restricted to 20% |
| Age allowance – single | £4,200 | for those aged 65-74 |
| Age allowance – additional | £2,665 | for married men aged 65-74. Relief restricted to 20% |
| Age allowance – single | £4,370 | over 75 years old |
| Age allowance – additional | £2,705 | over 75 years old. Relief restricted to 20% |

### National Insurance in 1994/95

| | | |
|---|---|---|
| Lower earnings limit | £57 | per week |
| Upper earnings limit | £430 | per week |
| Employee's contribution: | 2% | on first £57 |
| | 10% | on rest up to upper earnings limit |
| Employer's contribution | 10.2% | no upper limit |

If total earnings are less than £200 per week, then reduced rates of employer's contributions apply:

| | |
|---|---|
| 3.6% | £57-£99.99 |
| 5.6% | £100-£144.99 |
| 7.6% | £145-£199.99 |

## Tax rates in 1995/96

| | | |
|---|---|---|
| Lower rate income tax | 20% | applies to taxable income up to £3,200 |
| Basic rate income tax | 25% | applies to taxable income from £3,201 to £24,300 |
| Higher rate income tax | 40% | applies to taxable income over £24,301 |

## Allowances in 1995/96

| | | |
|---|---|---|
| Single personal allowance | £3,525 | |
| Additional (for married men or person with a dependent child) | £1,720 | relief restricted to 15% |
| Age allowance – single | £4,630 | for those aged 65-74 |
| Age allowance – additional | £2,995 | for married men aged 65-74. Relief restricted to 15% |
| Age allowance – single | £4,800 | over 75 years old |
| Age allowance – additional | £3,035 | over 75 years old. Relief restricted to 15% |

## National Insurance in 1995/96

| | | |
|---|---|---|
| Lower earnings limit | £58 | per week |
| Upper earnings limit | £440 | per week |
| Employee's contribution: | 2% | on first £58 |
| | 10% | on rest up to upper earnings limit |
| Employer's contribution | 10.2% | no upper limit |

If total earnings are less than £200 per week, then reduced rates of employer's contributions apply:

| | |
|---|---|
| 3% | £58 – £104.99 |
| 5% | £105 – £149.99 |
| 7% | £150 – £204.99 |

## National Insurance – Contracted Out Rates

Employee's contribution reduced by 1.8% on earnings between lower and upper earnings limit to 8.2%

Employer's contribution reduced by 3% to 7.2%

## Car Benefits

Taxable benefit based on list price up to a maximum of £80,000

| Business Mileage | Under 4 years | 4 years or over |
|---|---|---|
| 2,500 miles or less | 35% | 23.33% |
| 2,501-17,999 | 23.33% | 5.56% |
| 8,000 miles and over | 11.67% | 7.78% |

National insurance is also payable by the employer at 10.2% on the fuel scale charges as below.

## Car Fuel Scale Rates

| | 1994/95 | | 1995/96 | |
|---|---|---|---|---|
| Size of Car | Petrol | Diesel | Petrol | Diesel |
| Up to 1,400 cc | £640 | £580 | £670 | £605 |
| 1,401 cc to 2,000 cc | £810 | £580 | £850 | £605 |
| 2,001 cc or more | £1,200 | £750 | £1,260 | £780 |
| Without a cc | £1,200 | | £1,260 | |

## Fixed Profit Car Scheme

The non-profit rates for 1994/95 are:

| | to 4,000 miles in year | over 4,000 miles in year |
|---|---|---|
| Up to 1,000 cc | 27p | 15p |
| 1,001-1,500 cc | 33p | 19p |
| 1,501-2,000 cc | 41p | 23p |
| Over 2,000 cc | 56p | 31p |

Up-to-date rates available from local inspector of taxes.

# ANSWERS TO QUIZ

These are my suggested answers.

**1**   Ideally you should not be paying wages out of petty cash, but understandably a small amount may have to be paid from the petty cash tin.

The administrator should not sign the petty cash voucher herself, but should get the cleaner to sign it. At present, it would be possible for the cleaner to claim that he had not been paid and the administrator would have no evidence to show that she had left the money there.

The petty cash voucher should show the name of the cleaner and records should be kept of the cleaner's name and address.

The cleaner should have been asked to complete a form P46 when he first started work for the charity. If he had been able to sign the form to say that it was his main or only employment, then the form would just have to be kept with the payroll records. The amount of £40 is below the lower earnings limit for national insurance and below the tax threshold. If he could not sign, the completed form P46 would have to have been sent to the tax office to obtain the correct coding. The P46 should still be completed now, although late. Operate code BR until a coding is received from the tax office.

Because the deduction of tax will mean that the cleaner is worse off, we have to consider an increase in the rate of pay. Alternatively, we have to find someone who can legitimately work for £40 without deductions because they have no other work.

**2**   The state pension already uses up the personal allowances and so all earnings are subject to tax. Code BR will apply, although when they first start work, you should ask them to complete a P46, which should be sent to the tax office. Someone over pension age does not pay any employee's national insurance, however. Employer's national insurance is still payable.

**3**   A school-leaver will not usually have a P45 (assuming they have not had paid work before) and so they should be asked to complete a P46. You should put them onto the emergency code on a cumulative basis.

The school-leaver will not have a national insurance number and they should go to their local social security office to obtain one. They will need their birth certificate or similar identification.

**4** The potential liability for tax and national insurance on a lump sum of £500 paid to a self-employed consultant would be calculated as follows:

£500 is the net equivalent of £769.23 gross, assuming tax at 25% and national insurance at 10% should have been deducted.

| | |
|---|---:|
| Tax due at 25% on £769.23 | 192.31 |
| Employee's NI at 10% on £769.23 | 76.92 |
| Employer's NI at 10.2% on £769.23 | 78.46 |
| Total potential liability | 347.69 |

**5** Holiday pay and overtime pay are contractual payments and may not be paid as ex-gratia payments. If the employee does not work their notice, then the payment in lieu of notice is liquidated damages, not payment for work done. This part of the payment may be paid as an ex-gratia payment.

**6** **A)** Buying a season ticket for employees means that they are being given a benefit in kind. Because the benefit is the payment of the cost of travel between home and work, this will be taxable in full. The cost of the season ticket needs to be declared on the P11D by the employer and the employee's tax code will be adjusted in order to collect the tax due. No national insurance will be due, as a benefit has been given, not cash.

**B)** Lending money to employees interest-free to purchase a season ticket gives them the benefit of the saving on the interest. If the amount of the loan does not exceed £5,000, then the benefit will be ignored. Above £5,000 and the notional rates of interest issued by the Inland Revenue from time to time have to be used to calculate the value of the benefit. In practice, the details of the loan should be shown on the P11D and the Inland Revenue will calculate the benefit on the employee and tax them on it.

If any amount of the loan is written off, then this is a straightforward cash payment to the employee and it is taxable in full.

**C)** Giving an employee the cash to buy a season ticket would be seen as another form of remuneration. The cash should be added to the gross pay in the month when paid and tax paid accordingly. National insurance will also be due, as the cash would be included in the earnings figure on which NI contributions are calculated.

**7** The taxable benefit will be based on the manufacturer's price, plus the cost of extras. The road fund licence should be excluded, as this is part of the running costs. The amount £14,035 should therefore be the basis. So 35% of £14,035 should be calculated = £4,912.

As business miles exceed 2,500, this amount can be reduced by one third. (= £3,275)

As the fundraiser has only had the vehicle since 6 May 1994, the benefit may be reduced by one month, when the car was not available. (£3,275 x 11/12)

The taxable benefit is therefore £3,002.

---

**8** The total cost to the employer will include the cost of purchasing the vehicle, and the actual running costs of the vehicle. It will not cost the employer anything in tax; the taxable benefit gives rise to an additional tax burden on the employee. The employer will have to pay Class 1A national insurance contributions on the benefit. This will be an additional 10.2% of the benefit of £3,002 which is payable in one lump sum by 19 June of the following year.

---

**9** Any employer with high levels of SSP will be able to reclaim some of the SSP; if the SSP in a month is more than 13% of the total NI due for the month, then the excess SSP can be reclaimed.

---

**10** Volunteers should not be paid for attendance or for the work that they do. They may be reimbursed for expenses upon submission of a claim. The expenses could include travel from home to the charity, lunch and any other actual costs in the course of volunteering (e.g. telephone).

---

# REFERENCE MATERIAL

## Useful Guides and Leaflets from the Inland Revenue:

Employer's Basic Guide to PAYE (P8)

Employer's Further Guide to Pay As You Earn

Guide to Expenses Payments and Benefits for Directors and Certain Employees

Employed or Self-Employed?  Leaflet IR56

Expenses – forms P11D  Leaflet IR69

Students  Leaflet IR60

## Useful Guides and Leaflets from DSS Contributions Agency

Quick Guide to NIC, SSP, SMP (CA 27, previously NI 268)

Employer's Manual on National Insurance Contributions (Green Book 1)

Employer's Manual on SSP (Green Book 2)

Employer's Manual on SMP (Green Book 3)

Employer's Manual – Cars and Fuel (CA 33, previously NI 280)

NP18 Class 2 and 4 National Insurance for self employed people

NP 27A People with small earnings from self employment

NP23 Employer's Guide: Occupational pensions and contracting-out

NP29 Employer's guide to procedures on termination of contracted-out employment

NI 132 National Insurance for the employers of people working abroad

NI 35 National Insurance for company directors

## Useful Guides and leaflets from
## The Volunteer Centre UK

**All Expenses Paid?** – a short guide providing advice on policy and
procedure for voluntary organisations in this area.
£1.50 1992 edition ISBN 0 904647 82 X

**Volunteers in the Driving Seat – A Practical Guide for Volunteer
Drivers**
Guidance on the law, insurance and other areas as well as tax.
£1.50 1993 edition ISBN 1 897708 75 0

## Useful Guides from NCVO

**Duty Free? Payments for Charity Trustees – Trustee Briefing No.2**
written by Tim Gill and Kate Kirkland and available from NCVO. Price £3.00.
Guidance on the law and best practice for paying trustees for work done or
for expenses.

## Tolley's Guides

**Payroll Handbook**
Updated annually, this covers more than just the PAYE system and looks at
all aspects, including some employment law, pensions administration and
internal procedures.

**Income Tax**
Published annually just after the start of the new tax year, this is a
practitioner's guide to income tax law. It is divided by subject matter and
brings together relevant legislation and case law. With a good index, this is
a detailed reference book.

**National Insurance**
Published annually in line with tax years. A detailed reference book
covering all relevant legislation and case law.

# INDEX